THE CHALLENGE TO THE CHURCH

THE NIEMÖLLER-BLAKE CONVERSATIONS

———————————

THE CHALLENGE
TO THE CHURCH

THE NIEMÖLLER-BLAKE
CONVERSATIONS

LENT, 1965

EDITED BY
MARLENE MAERTENS

THE WESTMINSTER PRESS

PHILADELPHIA

LIBRARY OF CONGRESS CATALOG CARD No. 65-24514

Published by The Westminster Press ®
Philadelphia, Pennsylvania

PRINTED IN THE UNITED STATES OF AMERICA

SOLI DEO GLORIA

CONTENTS

ACKNOWLEDGMENTS

————————

Good friends helped me to bring this book into being. I am grateful to John M. Price for recording the sermons and dialogues, and to Lucile Degler and Dorothy Kurtz for transcribing the tapes and typing the manuscript. Kay Longcope gave editorial advice, as did the Reverend Drs. Longley, Pratt, and Leeman. The Reverends Paul and Elizabeth W. Fenske went over the entire manuscript with me and were very helpful.

But most of all, I want to thank Martin Niemöller and Eugene Carson Blake for having left this legacy with us.

M. M.

Philadelphia, Pennsylvania
May 8, 1965

PROLOGUE

How does one start a book such as this? There seems to be no need for an introduction—it stands on its own merits. On its pages are recorded a series of sermons and conversations delivered in Philadelphia, Commonwealth of Pennsylvania, in Lent, 1965, by two of the great religious leaders of our day, Martin Niemöller of Germany and Eugene Carson Blake of the United States of America. Whatever these two men have to say should make good reading for everyone who cares in terms of Christian responsibility about what happens in our world today, who desires to see the Word of God, the love of Christ, applied to all sorts and conditions of men.

How did it happen that they preached together and engaged in conversations for many of us in Philadelphia to hear, during one week in Lent, 1965? This is the story that needs to be told.

Somehow, at this moment, I see myself as that program chairman whom we all encounter at one time or another, who arises to announce with dignity that the speaker of the evening needs no introduction. But he does not sit down to let the speaker of the evening take over then and there. No, he remains on his feet for quite some time and eloquently proceeds with introducing the speaker who needs no introduction.

Invariably I have found a rewarding factor in this: the things then said did turn out to be worth knowing and are helpful in establishing a proper perspective for that which is to come. I fervently hope that this is true as I endeavor to tell it, thinking of that "love, which binds everything together in perfect harmony."

"Who is she who has so important a story to tell?" one might ask. The answer to this question is the beginning of this book.

I am a fellow Christian with all Christians in God's world, a fellow American with all Americans, and I am wide awake to what that means and entails. I am German born, brought up with great care to take my place in an honorable and responsible Christian society. However, the unfathomable vicissitude that befell Germany in National Socialism as it became Germany's law and enforced "saving" ideology placed me, for various reasons, among its prime targets. With my eyes wide open and all good senses intact, I walked through the very core of things. In doing so, I lost everything a human being can lose on this earth with one exception: I never asked God to spare my life, but he did.

Walking on with my hand in his, I became an American citizen by refuge, adoption, adaption, and indeed by love. Those experiences under National Socialism were not a nightmare to be forgotten, not a thing of the past from which I escaped to new shores: they were lessons from God, in his own ways, his call to take my stand in his Kingdom, a call from which there is no release.

For the past two thousand years the focal question of man's existence has been whether he will accept the love of Christ and live, live in the fullness of his truth, or refuse it and perish, perish by drifting into the abyss of man's ideologies, into nihilism. Throughout the ages, through many kinds of people and events, as indeed in our own century, history has witnessed to this truth. To me, to many of us who are alive today, that focal question has lost nothing of its momentum, and we know it never will. As we look about us, at the multitude of wide-open problems in our own country and in all the world, that question emerges with a new urgency and confronts us with the gravity of its claim upon us. It is God who asks this question, and we have to take our stand. We have to take our stand!

More than ever I thought on these things when I heard Martin Niemöller preach a Lenten sermon on "The Meaning of Jesus Christ in 1964" in the Episcopal cathedral at Newark, New Jersey. I had gone up from Philadelphia to hear him again and to visit for the few hours that he had to spare. Ours is an old friendship. He and my late husband were classmates in the German navy which they entered in 1910 as their life's career. My husband, from whom I was divorced perforce, under National Socialist legislature, remained in the active service of his country till he perished, three days before the Second World War's end, fighting the Russians as they entered Berlin.

Martin Niemöller changed from the iron cross to the cross of Christ, as I heard him put it once, after the end of the First World War. In 1924, he was ordained a Lutheran pastor.

It was this German pastor, bound to Christ, who stood up among us the very moment Adolf Hitler's anti-Christian ideology unmasked itself. His leadership in the Pastors' Emergency League and the Confessing Church are history. I, too, at its inception had become a part of the Confessing Church, which rejected and opposed National

Socialism as irreconcilable to the teachings of Jesus Christ and our faith in him.

In an unforgettable incident thirty years ago, in a moment of great need, Martin Niemöller steadied my faith. That class of 1910 of the German navy had gathered in Kiel, in northern Germany, for their twenty-fifth anniversary. There was much celebrating and many joys such as the reunion of old friends will provide. Yet, the situation was generally tense. The religious persecution was on many minds. We were not free to talk about it. We felt the heavy weight of our country's law-enforced new doctrine upon us. We were no longer free people in a free society.

Pastor Martin Niemöller, the senior of the class, ever faithful to old friends, had come to join us. Few people talked to him for fear of the very real dangers that his opposition to the Nazi government would cause for them. Others, who had long since grasped the deep significance of this opposition, wanted him to rest and relax among old friends. Quietly, he sat by my side and I, too, did not speak. But filled with fear and anxious questions about the future as I was, I could endure the silence just so long. Finally, I blurted out: "Dear Friend, please tell me, what do you think, what will happen, what is to become of us all, of our land. . . . Will the cause of Jesus Christ yet be victorious?"

Very slowly he lifted his head, looked up, then looked at me with deeply troubled eyes. But slowly they began to come alive, alive with warmth, with a smile, and with shining faith. He radiated the answer: *"You doubt—by any chance?"*

He did not doubt then, he did not doubt through eight years of concentration camp, nor did he doubt through those difficult years of the postwar reconstruction period. He does not doubt today, at seventy-three years of age and recently retired from leading the Evangelical Church in Hesse and Nassau for seventeen years and still leading and serving mankind as one of the presidents of the World Council of Churches. Wherever he goes, he follows Jesus Christ as Lord and Savior of us all, proclaims him as the only answer to our problems, and professes him to be the way, the truth, and the life.

At a luncheon following that service in Newark, Martin Niemöller told a few of his own experiences that became milestones to him in his growth toward ecumenicity. Some of them recur on the pages of this book. But the story he told me later that day became the nucleus of those thoughts that ultimately expressed themselves in that great week in Philadelphia, of which this book gives an account.

"Did you know," he mused, "that with all the traveling to the far corners of the world that I have done, it was not until last fall that I saw Rome for the first time in my life?" In a few days of leisure, Martin Niemöller, the tourist, took in as much of the Eternal City as he could. One day, he was "spotted" in St. Peter's, and then things happened very quickly. The Pope would like to see him—would he like to come?

The time for the visit was quickly set. Dr. Niemöller described the details with warmth and emotion. In the Pope's antechamber, Cardinal Bea joined him to take him in. The door was opened, and the two men entered.

At this moment, suspense got the better of me. "Martin," I said, in Protestant mock horror, "you did not kneel to kiss the ring?"

"I could not if I would have wanted to," he replied. "The Pope came toward me, both hands outstretched. He smiled gently as he greeted me, 'How glad I am finally to meet the man for whom I have prayed these many years.' "

And so they joined hands, Pope Paul VI and Pastor Martin Niemöller, brothers of the faith.

It is amazing, it seems to me, how big things at times become little things, and little things all of a sudden grow to tremendous proportions. We reach for the stars and then find that their radiance is right among us!

I knew then that I wished to share this story with many friends, this story of the simplicity of our oneness in Christ. "I wish you'd come to Philadelphia next Lent," I told him, "and tell this story and all the others. We need to hear them to make us earnestly want unity and not get lost in an outward search!"

It was quite natural that at that moment we should speak of Eugene Carson Blake, well known to us all as the Stated Clerk of The United Presbyterian Church in the United States of America. To Martin Niemöller, he is also a fellow worker in the World Council of Churches and more than that, a good friend. Differing in age, background, upbringing, and, indeed, experiences in life, from different countries and in different tongues, they yet speak the same language as they proclaim, through thick and thin, the only answer to man's sin, confusion, problems, and utter need: the Word of God, Jesus Christ and his love.

Dr. Blake's prophetic call to unite in one body several of our American denominations, to join hands in one church, truly catholic, truly evangelical, and truly reformed, is above all else a charge to a new spirit within us. His intrepid stand for equal rights before the law for all Americans marks him clearly as one who practices what he preaches.

"Martin," I said to my friend, "how wonderful it would be if together you both would preach to us in Philadelphia on the burning issues of our day. . . ."

"Why don't you try and arrange it?" smiled my friend as he stepped into the car that was to take him to Kennedy Airport.

"Why don't you try and arrange it?" My heart began to hammer at the thought on the way back to Philadelphia.

It is true, with that background of mine I have been led to feel increasingly uncomfortable recently with what I would like to call a complacent quality to our Christian life. With our many churches and various organizations buzzing with work and involved in full schedules of services of worship, meetings, and activities, we have lulled ourselves into the comfortable conclusion that we are being good Christians. Figuratively speaking, we are inclined to sing "Stand Up, Stand Up for Jesus" with joyful vigor. We shake the minister's hand at the door and tell him, "I have enjoyed the sermon." We chat with friends, welcome newcomers, agree on the time of this week's meetings, and are generally pleasant with our neighbor. We go home, turn on the news, *and sit down.* And we remain seated, so to speak, till next Sunday.

"Why don't I try?" The thought turned to prayer.

The Reverend Dr. Cuthbert Pratt was the first person to whom I spoke. He is the rector of The Church of the Holy Trinity (Episcopal) on Rittenhouse Square, my own church. He liked what he heard and suggested that we consult with his predecessor, the Reverend Dr. Harry Longley, now retired and free from everyday parish duties. He, too, liked what he heard, and both men agreed that we should get together as many center city churches as

would want to have part in this. And to me they said, "Try
and get Dr. Blake!"

By the time we "got Dr. Blake," the World Council of
Churches' New York office, through our good friend
Eleanor Kent Browne, had allotted us the only time avail-
able on Dr. Niemöller's already crowded schedule for
Lent, 1965. Happily, Holy Trinity confirmed the invitation,
the time, and the place. We were on the way.

In early June, a small group of center city ministers
gathered in Dr. Blake's office. At that meeting I was asked
for an outline—what did I think that week should entail?
Background and motivation of the plan by now were clear.
And so I spoke of my hopes for a great rally of Philadelphians under the Word of God given long ago but just as
relevant today. I spoke of the letter in the book of Revelation that begins, "And to the angel of the church of Philadelphia write . . ." and that we, having received the letter
simply would take it from there. I spoke of a concurring
thought that had to do with Walter Russell Bowie's great
hymn, "Lord Christ, when first thou cam'st to men, upon
a cross they bound thee." This hymn, with its relevant
text, should be our guiding song each day—our theme
hymn.

At that meeting Eugene Carson Blake committed himself to our plan. It was a great moment when we watched
him drawing a line through the week March 15 to 19,
1965, in his calendar and writing the word "Philadelphia"
into the space.

In our group that day was the Reverend Dr. William
Powell, the General Secretary of the Greater Philadelphia
Council of Churches. From the beginning we had hoped to
win the Council's sponsorship, not, however, to hand over
a good idea to a good organization to do our work, but

rather, to let the Council be the expression of a new, unorganizational community undertaking.

Not long after, Dr. Powell brought the Council's commitment. Great was our joy! Dr. Longley agreed to be the general chairman; Dr. Pratt, program chairman; and the Reverend Dr. William O. Moyer, pastor of the Holy Communion Lutheran Church, publicity chairman.

At first, the going was tough. We wanted to include everybody in center city who wanted to be included. But it took an average of five telephone calls to reach a busy center city minister to invite him to a meeting only to hear him say, "Sorry, I can't come, I have another meeting." Accordingly, the initial planning was not altogether encouraging. The Reverend Dr. J. Ernest Somerville, minister of the First Presbyterian Church, Holy Trinity's good friend and neighbor, summed up some of these initial difficulties:

Some of us involved in the planning felt that there were many factors that seemed to work against the possible success of the meetings. It was the wrong time, both of the year and of the day; it was not in the most favorable location; the planning committees changed in composition at every meeting; proxy votes were used or rejected seemingly by whim. That it even had a measure of response was surely testimony that it had something of the Spirit in it.

It was the outreach for a great goal, the uniqueness of a new undertaking without the cogs-in-the-wheel services of existing organizations, that caused these initial difficulties. We were aware of these difficulties, knew that we had to work them out, and were willing to do so. Dr. Powell had this to say:

Ways of presenting the good news that will attract the thoughtful Christian and intrigue the seeker after truth only arise infrequently. Often when they do, there are factors of time, space, and convenience that threaten to destroy their execution. Such was the situation when Mrs. Maertens approached ministers of our center city churches and the Council's staff. The obstacles in the way: the conflict with long-range Lenten practices and commitments, the availability of the key persons on a fixed schedule, and the insertion of yet another series of meetings into already full plans seemed too much. But as one by one adjustments were made and enthusiasm grew, the idea gradually took hold and proved in its final execution to meet a need in a time and a place for which no other answer had been offered.

Step by step, our local planning took shape. We soon realized that there was no need for a clear division between program and publicity: we worked together as best we could. More and more we were captivated by a spiritual urgency to our planning. Dr. Pratt expressed it thus:

To plan, to prepare, to coordinate—these are duties often deemed drudgery; but for these services that was far from the case. The opportunity was a far, far different one than that. What was attempted was to provide a setting in which men and women with minds attuned to God might hear, above all else, his voice and begin to understand his will for a city— both theirs and his—anew. Given this vision of what was to be done, the rest consisted of making the setting as simple as possible and the participation as complete as possible. This we were able to do.

Of course, we were still a long way off from this accomplishment. There was drudgery, but we loved it. In November, I consulted with Dr. Niemöller in Germany to get his thoughts on paper and to coordinate them to our Philadelphia plans. In December, on behalf of the Committee, I met with Dr. Blake in his office and brought him up to date. For some moments he looked over the papers that I had spread out for him. Then he looked up with a broad smile. "Let's call it 'An Open Letter to Philadelphia.' What do you say?"

I said, "Amen." At this meeting he crystallized the topics for each day out of all the earlier suggestions, summarizing them as "The Issues and Opportunities Facing the Church of Jesus Christ." He agreed with Martin Niemöller that the text from Revelation should be read the first day only, and that the sermons on the subsequent days should be placed under separate texts. These he wanted to select with Martin Niemöller, whom he would see at Enugu, Nigeria, at the World Council of Churches' meeting in mid-January. Finally, he suggested that we should arrange for a public dinner after the service on Friday at which the people could ask questions and generally voice what they had to say.

On January 26, 1965, I received a letter from Dr. Blake, handwritten at the airport of Lagos, Nigeria, on the twenty-third and mailed in San Francisco on the twenty-fifth. It contained the passages from Holy Scripture, the texts for the sermons of both men for each of the five days. Together they had selected them at Enugu, Nigeria.

These passages later were read each day during the brief opening service of worship. I am slightly getting ahead of the story now as I list the names of the ministers in charge of these services. They were the Right Reverend Robert L. DeWitt, D.D., Bishop, Protestant Episcopal Diocese of Pennsylvania, Monday; the Reverend Samuel E. Kidd, D.D., President, Eastern Pennsylvania Synod, Lutheran Church in America, Tuesday; the Reverend John D. Bright, D.D., Bishop, First Episcopal District, African Methodist Episcopal Church, Wednesday; the Reverend H. G. Gearhart, Minister, Third Christian Church and

President of the Greater Philadelphia Council of Churches, Thursday; and the Reverend Philip W. Weiss, Minister, Bethany United Church of Christ and Moderator, Philadelphia Association, Friday.

The benediction was pronounced from the altar as each service ended. Each minister selected one verse from Holy Scripture that would sum up the wealth of thought of his particular day. Those who thus served were: the Reverend J. Ernest Somerville, D.D., Minister, First Presbyterian Church, Monday; the Reverend Frederick Isaacksen, Rector, St. Luke and the Epiphany (Episcopal), Tuesday; the Reverend Brian Kingslake, Associate Minister, The Church of the New Jerusalem, Wednesday; the Reverend Frederick A. Maser, D.D., Minister, St. George's Methodist Church, Thursday; and the Reverend (Mrs.) Elizabeth W. Fenske, United Church of Christ and Protestant Minister to Drexel Institute of Technology, Friday.

There was one final, happy chore left to do: the selection of proper hymns best suited to be sung each day. It was the Reverend Judson S. Leeman, M.D., the Associate Rector of The Church of the Holy Trinity, who hereto contributed his great knowledge, wisdom, and taste. Looking back on our work, he had this to say:

We wanted to sing hymns whose words rightly expressed full Christian ideas about the subjects of concern, yet whose music was good and singable though not necessarily "familiar." With some trepidation we did just that and experienced the joyful response of the congregations as they joined in real spirited singing day by day.

The program was now complete. Its structure remained the same each day: the hymn, the service, announcements, the theme hymn, the sermon-dialogues, the closing hymn, and the benediction.

Publicity took shape. Chairman Dr. Moyer, in close co-operation with Dr. Powell and his efficient Council of Churches' apparatus, Kay Longcope, Associate Director of the Presbyterian Office of Information in New York, and the Reverend H. Francis Hines, Executive Director of the Philadelphia Council of Churches' Department of Broad-casting, got very busy. Two thousand churches in our area were informed of the forthcoming great event and the general public alerted. The "Open Letter to Philadelphia" was on its way.

We had planned and prepared with care and with love, down to the minutest detail. The one thing we could not "prepare" was the attendance. Monday morning, March 15, 1965, Dr. Longley, the general chairman, and I waited at Philadelphia's Thirtieth Street Station for Martin Niemöller's train to get in. Slightly apprehensive, I asked my friend, "Harry, how are you going to feel this after-noon in case there will be one hundred people in Holy Trinity?"

His answer came quickly. "That'll be ninety-seven over the basic requirement," he said earnestly.

I thought of that in the afternoon when I walked across Rittenhouse Square toward Holy Trinity with those two men, Martin Niemöller and Eugene Carson Blake. I thought of how many times and at how many places they had walked together on the road, serving their Lord in mankind—two or three together in his name. Now, for a brief and unforgettable moment, I walked along with them.

As we approached the church, we saw people arriving in great numbers. More than one half hour before the service began that "ninety-seven beyond the basic require-ment" was more than doubled.

Dr. Pratt and Dr. Longley greeted our guests and took them to the sacristy for vesting.

Then, Frederick Roye, our organist, had a special welcome for our visitors. He put his hands to the keyboard and gently played those great Lenten hymns we all have in common. Before the first service began on Monday, March 15, 1965, we were one great fellowship of love, and our Lord was in the midst of us.

In his name, the "Open Letter to Philadelphia" was ready to be delivered.

AN OPEN LETTER TO PHILADELPHIA

CHAPTER ONE

THE OPEN DOOR

Text: Revelation 3:7–13
Monday, March 15

DR. BLAKE BEGAN

As some of you may know, I was born in St. Louis, Missouri, as was my father before me. In the autumn of 1917, when I was eleven years old, my father and my mother took my sister, my brother, and me to Washington, D.C., to live. The reason for this first move of my family from the Middle West to the Eastern seaboard was the entrance of our nation into World War I, allied as we were with Great Britain and France against imperial Germany, headed by Kaiser Wilhelm II, its emperor. My father was in the steel business, became a dollar-a-year man in government service, an employee of the Steel Distribution Committee of the Federal Government, a rather small operation in that war contrasted with how we learned to do it thirty years later.

I mention these personal matters at the beginning of these dialogue sermons, in which I feel it is a great honor and privilege to participate with my dear and distinguished friend, Dr. Martin Niemöller, because I want to remind you that in that same year, 1917, Martin Niemöller was an officer on a U-boat in the imperial German navy.

How bizarre that he and I, nearly fifty years later, should be speaking to you from the same pulpit as Christian ministers under obedience to the same sovereign Lord —even Jesus Christ. And add to the surprise, if you will, that it is an Episcopal pulpit from which we speak, since he is a Lutheran pastor and I have been, from my Baptism, a Presbyterian.

In 1917, I had not heard of Martin Niemöller; much less had he heard of me. But those hectic war years in Washington made me very conscious of imperial Germany and its emperor, whom we saw only in caricature as a sort of Adolf Hitler of an earlier generation. And though I did not know the roster of the submarine officers of the German navy, even at eleven years of age I was, as were all Americans, highly conscious of the U-boat, whose unrestricted campaign against merchant shipping was the stated reason for our entrance into that "European War," an entrance on the side of Great Britain and France, and against Germany.

Now the question that I want you to ponder with me is this: What has happened in these five decades to put us together in this church, me with Martin Niemöller? For I was taught early to hate his nation, to ridicule his emperor, and to detest all that he was fighting for, and particularly to despise the "new barbarism" that the U-boat warfare symbolized, revealing, for all the world to see, the naked evil of the Huns, as we in those days described the German people. Had I been a little older, I too would doubtless have served this nation in its Armed Forces. One of us could have been put in the place to kill the other. What has happened to us, and to the church, and to the world, to make these dialogue sermons possible?

In a word, the answer is that the ecumenical movement has so transformed my Christian understanding that I am more interested to hear today what this German Lutheran Martin Niemöller will say to this my city of Philadelphia in the name of Jesus Christ than I would be to hear almost any other preacher or pastor in all the world. As an American Christian, I hope you will listen to him most carefully, for I believe we need here in the very churches of Philadelphia, and in all our nation, to hear and heed what God will say to us through this man.

Now, when the author of Revelation wrote his book, it was precisely at the moment that for the first time Christianity was moving out of the confines and limitations of one nation and one culture (that of Israel) into the Oikoumenē, "the whole inhabited world," with its many languages, its separate histories, and its varied faiths. The letters to the seven churches of Asia, which comprise the whole of the second and third chapters of this strange book, are in part at least symbolic of a new wholeness and a new transcendence that the author was pressing upon the new young churches then. And now, after nearly two millennia, what God said through the author of the book of Revelation to all the churches then is exactly what he is saying now to the churches, churches no longer new, churches, however, that are threatened with apostasy today, apostasy in forms caused sometimes by their ancient traditions and their rootage in separate and limited cultures. The open door about which we speak, the open door before our churches, is our opportunity to move with boldness in the name of Jesus Christ out into an open sea of an ecumenical movement in a frail craft with a cross for the mast, leaving the safe moorings in the protected harbors of our past.

The letter to the church in Philadelphia, a small city of Asia Minor, becomes the basic text of this series of dialogue sermons here in this Philadelphia of the new world. It begins: "And to the angel [or better, messenger] of the church in Philadelphia write: 'The words of the holy one, the true one, who has the key of David, who opens and no one shall shut, who shuts and no one opens. I know your works. Behold, I have set before you an open door, which no one is able to shut.'"

In these fifty years, the sovereign God of all the earth has set before the church—and all our churches—an open door. He has opened it. No man can shut it. He can shut it. He does not force our churches through it. The churches can, if they will, pretend that the door is closed. They can refuse to leave the cozy hearths of their household gods. But the ecumenical movement in our time is an open door. And it is not yet clear whether the churches of Philadelphia, or of any city in the world, quite dare to walk boldly through that door in faith. Nor is it clear how long that door will remain open to us, as it is today. For God, who is the God of history, the God of the history of ancient Israel (he has the key of David) and of all the separate histories of the varied peoples of the six continents, this God has opened the door in our times as earlier he opened it for Paul and Barnabas when they first embarked from Antioch consciously to share Jesus Christ, son of David and Son of God, with the whole inhabited world. At that time God opened the door by employing the given unity of the Greek language and culture and the given order of the Roman Empire.

Often the twentieth century has been described by dis-
illusioned and discouraged men simply as a century of two
great wars with another still greater threatening, and as a
century of political, economic, moral, and social collapse.
Our century may truly be so described. But not *simply* so.
For in this shaking century, God has opened a door before
his church, a door that has been blocked for millennia.
The world has entered a new era of universal history. The
church in Philadelphia, or in any city in the whole world,
can no longer isolate herself from the Christian church
of any nation. The church exists in Europe and in the
Americas. The church lives and witnesses in Africa, Aus-
tralia, Asia, and the islands of the sea. The church survives
in China and in the U.S.S.R., in Eastern Europe, in Vene-
zuela, Spain, and Cuba. And we are free, as we were in
1917, to suppose that God has no witnesses in "enemy"
lands. We may write off Indonesia and the Congo, for separate reasons, but we may write them off, if we will.
Though the door is open, God does not push us through it.
But God has opened the door into the whole inhabited
world by the ecumenical movement under the Lord Jesus
Christ, and my plea to you in Philadelphia here this week
is that we do not shut our eyes to that door which is open
before us now.

One word more must be said to complete my part of this
opening dialogue. So far I have spoken of this open door
as if it were beckoning us simply across geographical lines
and walls, across political and cultural differences, and so
it is. But now I would remind you that God has been as
active in his church as he has been active in his world in
this half century. This action is symbolized by the fact I
mentioned at the outset, that it is a Lutheran and a Presbyterian pastor who address you, members of our denom-

inations but members, I am sure, of many others, and we address you in an Episcopal church. If our world has been shaken by God's action in these five decades of world history, no less has been the revolutionary shaking of the structures of the church of Jesus Christ itself.

Not for four hundred and fifty years has God opened the door so widely to his church in the West. Not for a thousand years has he beckoned through so wide an open door to his church in the East as well as in the West.

Yet how easy it is for all of us to turn our backs upon the door to Christian unity and to busy ourselves with our denominational games, nourished by our past prejudices, and at a moment when the divisions of the beleaguered church militant are crying for unified command of Jesus Christ to withstand the forces of atheism, skepticism, hatred, and confusion with which the church is faced.

The ecumenical movement gives us opportunity then to move out boldly, if we will, through God's open door, not only across political and geographic divisions of a deeply divided world, but also across those sometimes higher walls, sharp-spiked, of the division of the church in all these local places, like Philadelphia, where Christians live, and work, and witness in their way to their Lord.

The World Council of Churches in 1961 at New Delhi, in India, adopted a statement that characterized the essential lineaments of a united church as one, and I quote:

"We believe that the unity which is both God's will and his gift to his Church is being made visible as all in each place who are baptized into Jesus Christ and confess him as Lord and Saviour are brought by the Holy Spirit into one fully committed fellowship, holding the one apostolic faith, preaching the one Gospel, breaking the one bread, joining in common prayer, and having a corporate life reaching out in witness and service to all and who at the same time are united with the whole Christian fellowship in all places and all ages in such wise that ministry and members are accepted by all, and that all can act and speak together as occasion requires for the tasks to which God calls his people."

That vision, I need not remind you, despite all the progress of these fifty years, is still a distant goal. Our Roman Catholic friends have just begun to talk with us and we with them, and both of us are very awkward in that dialogue. But it is through the door that God himself has opened in our time that we may view with hope even that distant goal. It is through the open door that God calls us now to walk.

DR. NIEMÖLLER CONTINUED

Surely, my Christian friends, the door behind which we Christians, as our Father's family, assemble and live in fraternal fellowship, in which Jesus the Christ spreads his Spirit as "the first-born among many brethren," is no longer barred. It never was; but when Jesus had left his disciples, they came together, and "the doors were shut . . . for fear of the Jews," as we are told in John's Gospel. Yet, we are told also that Jesus did not acknowledge their seclusion but that he "came . . . and stood in the midst," saying, "Peace be unto you." And there in the room that they had locked, he gave them his missionary mandate: "As my Father hath sent me, even so send I you." He opened the door!

Whenever and wherever the Christian church becomes aware of her weakness and her minority character, the temptation arises to shut and bar the doors to feel safe and —if possible at all—to save her life. This has happened in the history of the church quite a number of times; it always means a real and dangerous temptation; and in spite of the high valuation that the Christian church experiences and enjoys in certain parts of our world today, there is also this strong countercurrent of which most Christians are not even aware but which carries them—and maybe ourselves—along, when we thoughtlessly speak of people as "still going to church," "still having their children baptized," "still being Christians." "Still"—as if all this soon would be finished!

This being true, and I do think no one can deny it, we certainly ought to be on our guard when we become aware of "open doors." They may mean new chances for expanding Christian influence and effect in many, if not in all, parts of the world, and they may mean also a fruit-bearing exchange and communication among Christian communities and churches. The evolution of the ecumenical movement proceeds, to some extent at least, from this hope and expectation. But on the other hand, we know of Christian groups also who have their doubts and their hesitations with regard to these undeniably open doors, for they may be just as well open doors for the intrusion of adversaries and enemies, who intend and try to fight against, destroy, dissolve, and poison the body of Christ, to catch and to scatter the sheep. And we are warned of "false prophets, which come to you in sheep's clothing, but inwardly they are ravening wolves," or as it is expressed in our text, "the synagogue of Satan who say that they are Jews"—the people of God—"and are not, but lie." We must not pass by this problem. We have to face the decisive fact that the door before us has been opened wide so that we, the churches, can reach out and go to nearly "all people that on earth do dwell." We can associate with one another regardless of our traditional separations and still remaining differences in faith and order, and in doctrine and structure. As a church that wants to be genuinely Christian, we must face what this fact means to us, and what conclusions we have to draw from it. The answer is not just a matter of course, and the "open door" actually can be both a call to activity and action or a call to deliberation and cautiousness. Probably it must be both, for every chance has also a temptation with it, and it is up to us to take and to fulfill this chance and to resist and to reject the temptation.

Yet, there is one consequence we have to draw from the Lord's intervention, from his action by which he has set this open door before us and his church, that gives us access to nations and races and also to our sister churches. We must pass through it and go out; we must not stay when and where we are settled peacefully and securely. This kind of peace and security is deceptive and dangerous because it is based on a widespread, yet treacherous, superstition. It makes us believe that to do nothing means to commit no sin, no crime, no injustice. We ought to know better. Jesus Christ, our Lord, will judge his people for their omissions: "Inasmuch as ye did it not to one of the least of these, ye did it not to me." The open door is his call for passing through and for going out; but we must do this not in self-confidence nor in trusting in what seems to be a good and favorable opportunity, for this can easily turn out to be the temptation of which we are being warned. There is one only who will keep us "from the hour of temptation," and he is willing to do it for the church in Philadelphia, considering her "little strength," but also her faithfulness: "Thou . . . hast kept my word, and hast not denied my name!" This must continue, and no success must induce and seduce her to forget whom she is meant to serve: "Hold that fast which thou hast, that no man take thy crown."

Christendom has had and has enjoyed the "open door" for many centuries, and the results of Christian activity and influence are obvious in what we call culture and civilization. We do think highly of what has been achieved in science and scholarship, in literature and arts, in learning and education, and in many other fields; and nearly everywhere in the "Christian world" the traces of Christian contribution in all fields of personal and social human life can be found and shown.

At the same time we cannot but admit that also the omissions and deficiencies are obvious in our "Christian world," that our fathers and we ourselves have not been able to "overcome" the tempting power of our own achievements. We Christians have gone out through the open door, we have paid our contribution, and then we have retired again and gone back through the open door into our own house of religious enjoyment and peace. The problem is: Do we, as Christians, in going out really keep the Master's word and not deny his name? Or do we go out on our own, handing over to others only those gifts and advices of the Lord which were accepted as agreeable and reasonable? In other words, did they then and do we now, in passing through the "open door," follow Jesus Christ; did they, and do we, walk and work in his presence and under his control and direction? For everything that the church does and that is not in concordance with his will and Spirit therefore will not find his approval and support. It will have no salutary effect, but instead will do harm or fade away.

Accordingly, our first concern, when being faced with the open door as we are today in our fellowship of the

World Council of Churches, must be that we do not stay behind on our own for safety's sake. This would mean suicide, for "whosoever will save his life shall lose it"! We have to go out following our Lord's command: "Go ye into all the world." We owe the gospel message to all men whom we can reach, and we must see to it that we fulfill according to the Scriptures our common calling with all who confess Jesus Christ as God and Savior.

But this, then, is our second and our decisive concern, that we must not go our own way. When we have passed through the "open door," we shall be lost and work in vain if we trust our own reasoning and planning and ability without keeping our Lord's command, "Follow me, for without me ye cannot do anything." This temptation to do without him has proved fatal in the past, and it certainly has not declined in its fatality. Surely, when reference is being made in our text to a special moment of grave temptation—"the hour of temptation, which shall come upon all the world"—in which the church of Christ Jesus will need to be kept and in which she is being admonished not to give way, but to hold on, then I am convinced that this occurs in every Christian's life and that each one of us knows it when we survey the way we have come. I also think that every generation of the Christian church has to pass through its special hour of temptation, and that therefore we must remain alerted to it to recognize, early and clearly, the threat from which we need to be kept, so that the church will not become its victim unaware. It is a very narrow ridge on which the church, in the discipleship of Jesus Christ, is meant to follow her Master!

In our generation we have come to recognize once more that the Christian church must not restrict herself to man's religious needs. The church has been misled in this direction. She has regarded herself—especially where she be-

came a state church or a more or less national church—
liable only for her people's relationship with God and his
transcendental world. Christianity, as a religion of one
among many, may be even the best one, but has no direct
connection with and no direct influence upon the other
spheres of human individual and social life. These must be
left to their own innate laws and rules, as they are different
from the religious person's ethical and moral code. Society
has its own rules and seeks and develops its corresponding
code in the field of economics and science, education and
pedagogics, politics and diplomacy. In all these fields the
Christian church, in a great part of our world, had become
disinterested until she became aware again of her share
and specific responsibility that cannot be detached and
severed as long as she really lives.

But how to do it? Evidently we cannot change society,
education, politics, and economics to make them "Christian"; that would call for all people to be Christians and
live in faith. According to Paul, this is impossible, as he
wrote to the Christian church in Thessalonica: "For *all*
men have not faith." Yet, we have to offer them what our
Lord recommends to those who listen to his advice and we
—his church, his followers, his disciples—must help to put
into effect as much of it as possible. And here the great
temptation lies in wait for us and the whole church. As we
go through the open door and deal with our fellowmen
and all their need and distress, we are being tempted to
make plans and programs such as we, according to our own
judgment, believe to be practicable.

Without any doubt we must do so, but we must also be
mindful that these plans are nothing more than our con-
tributions, and only meant to serve our fellows, to protect
them from such harm as can be avoided, and to remove

misfortune, grief, and pain. However, we must beware of mistaking our principles and actions for Christianity itself. The faith cannot be regarded as a system of principles in which we believe, principles that are nothing more than superstition. Christian faith means to belong to Jesus, the Christ and the Lord, to live in communion with him, to follow in his footsteps, and therefore to act in his spirit, to ask him what he wants us to do, and to receive from him what we need to fulfill his calling. He has promised, "My strength is made perfect in weakness."

The church has to overcome the temptation of separating herself from the source of her life and going her own way. This may look successful for a while, but it will end in frustration, loneliness, and death: "Hold that fast which thou hast, that no man"—not even thou thyself—"take thy crown."

THE DIALOGUE

After the first two sermons had been preached, there were but a few minutes left of what had been planned as an "hour-long service." As the two churchmen drew closer together to begin their first exchange, we found that no one was restless, no one left.

Dr. Blake posed the first question: "Martin, there are people who really feel that the ecumenical movement, if it is referred to at all in The Revelation to John, is the synagogue of Satan. They feel that the ecumenical movement presses against the truth that our several churches have received in the past. How do you, a Lutheran, a German Lutheran pastor of a church that is known for the sharp articulation of its faith in confessions, really work with us in the ecumenical movement without being drawn away from your faith, with all our Anglo-Saxon fuzziness and the American pragmatism—and I won't even mention some of the worst theologized variations that are even bad from my point of view?"

Dr. Niemöller replied: "I am not so deeply convinced that theology really answers those questions to which we must seek an answer. Theology and doctrine may be just as bad as what you call 'fuzziness' in American and English Christianity. To me, the point is quite different. As a son of the Westphalian diaspora—in my youth, Protestants were a minute minority in that part of Germany—I remained deeply opposed to any kind of Roman Catholicism until God brought me together in a concentration camp with three Roman Catholic priests. There it happened that each morning we prayed the breviary together, read the Protestant and Catholic Bibles together, and Greek and Hebrew in the afternoon. Finally, when we were freed after having lived thus together for two and one half years, we began corresponding with each other and signed these letters, 'Your Brother in Christ.' And so it came to me that their faith is not different from my faith.

"I really think that someone who believes in Jesus Christ and puts all his trust in him has a personal relationship to him, calls him 'My Lord,' and asks each and every day, 'What wilt thou have me to do; what shall I do? Do go with me through this day so that I do not go my own ways and wrong ways.' I believe that this is much more important for Christians who want to work together than any theological or psychological or otherwise seemingly important difference may be."

Dr. Blake said, with a smile: "I think I stimulated you to say what I wanted you to say. Isn't it true that one of the things that pulled you and the Roman Catholic priests together was your common use of the Scriptures? I have

been to all kinds of Christian conferences from my boy-
hood until today, excepting, of course, a prison camp. In
all of that experience there has been no place where we
were not drawn together by the Scriptures. The Scriptures
we do have in common! As I have sat and listened to
representatives of the Eastern Orthodox churches and of
the Anglicans and of all kinds and varieties of churches,
there was not one of them in the fellowship of the ecumenical movement who was willing to say, 'My place, my
position, is *not* supported by the Word of God as we find
it in the Bible.' "

Dr. Blake looked at his watch. Time was running out,
but he asked one more question, of special significance:

"What do you think, Martin: Is the ecumenical movement as much a movement for the renewal of the church
—meaning the church really beginning to follow Jesus
Christ in a new and fresh way—as it is interested in the
unity of the church?"

Dr. Niemöller replied: "I think that the most important
event in the history of the ecumenical movement during
the last decades, from my point of view in Germany, was
the integration into the World Council of Churches of the
International Missionary Council. This really went down
to what we call the grass roots. And now people are really
interested in what is happening to Christianity, not so
much in an ecumenical organization but in what is the
common calling of Christianity in which all of us have to
take our stand. We are not talking about something that
is happening between the organizations and their leadership. It is, rather, something to which everybody is being
called. This begins to break forth, to produce fruit, and
that is exactly what we hope for the future of the Christian church in this our world—that it really becomes a wit-

ness. You know as well as I do that the importance of the Bible to Protestants is its witness to the man Jesus of Nazareth being God's Christ and our Savior, and that this is the Word of God that we have to find in the Bible, which was made flesh in the One whom we call Lord."

CHAPTER TWO

CHRIST FOR THE WORLD

TEXT: COLOSSIANS 1:15–23
Tuesday, March 16

DR. NIEMÖLLER BEGAN

This text from The Letter of Paul to the Colossians may seem to us rather strange and enigmatic at first sight, because we are no longer accustomed to the atmosphere that it makes us breathe. In our generation everything, the whole of life, has become relative. Nothing remains fixed, stable, and consistent. So, instinctively we shrink back from everything that claims absolute and universal validity, and also from everybody who pretends to be of general and universal authority. As the old Greek proverb says: "Everything is flowing, changing, developing; nothing stays what it is or where it is—such is life." Of this dynamic character of all that is and happens, we have become aware more clearly than any generation before, since due to the speed of these changes nobody is able to escape, nobody is able to withdraw into a sphere of quiet, shelter, and protection. Accordingly, we no longer trust—at least, we are no longer inclined to trust—in any pretension that claims to be recognized unconditionally, totally, and universally. I even think that our antipathy to communism and our dislike of the communist ideology stem mainly from its claim to universal acknowledgment. It wants to dominate the whole of mankind and to this end proclaim a "world revolution." This fact is sufficient for most of us to reject communism: there is no need to study it more thoroughly. That it wants all men, universally and totally, is sufficient, and that settles the point.

Today's topic, as well as today's text, reminds us that the Christian church stands in the midst of our world with a corresponding claim. We may not have become conscious of it until recently; we took it as a matter of fact, living in the Christian part of our globe and having been brought up in the traditional understanding, that this whole world just will have to become Christian. What may have seemed normal and right to us certainly makes a very different impression on others. Without any doubt we Christians want to see all mankind becoming Christians. But such endeavors have met with considerable opposition and rejection, first of all from our own people. Living in a more or less "Christian world," our own people did not share the general belief that to spread Christianity to non-Christian peoples would mean a blessing; but instead it might even bring harm to them. Becoming Christians would separate them from their inherited culture and nationhood and accordingly from their fellow countrymen, their family, tribe, and race. This effect became widely spread, and when these peoples began to become autonomous, this criticism was publicly expressed. Today quite a number of them refuse and fight Christianity with just the same general argument with which we are fighting communism: a new ideology, not our own, is being recommended to us, even forced upon us from the outside. It claims to be universal; therefore, it is being rejected as not conformable to our culture and not to be accepted.

In spite of these adverse attitudes and negative commentaries, the church through all centuries has stuck to the absolute and universal claim of the apostolic message: there is no other Savior and Christ except Jesus of Nazareth, and he is "the same yesterday and today and for ever"; "neither is there salvation in any other: for there is none other name under heaven given among men, whereby we must be saved." This is to say that this man Jesus is recognized by his apostles and by his followers as the very center of God's creation; there is nothing from its very beginning unto its fulfillment that is not dependent on him. "All things were created through him and for him." He is the one entitled to say: "I am Alpha and Omega, the beginning and the end." Thus his church understands and explains its mandate and commission to make Jesus known "to all creatures." And whereas all other religions are limited, this man is proclaimed as "Lord of all," as the one "Savior of all the world." Here, then, no room is left for relativity, for any other concept or a variety of ideas and ideals: Jesus the Nazarene, a member of the Jewish people, the Messiah, in whom "all the promises of God"—as announced to his chosen people of old—"are yea, and in him Amen." He is "Christ for the World."

My friends, we know that this claim to universal and total significance and validity is made not only by the communist ideology and by the Christian gospel, but that other religions and philosophies of life lay claim to the same efficacy and importance. That makes it necessary for us to examine the basic argumentation of such a claim.

These various religions and philosophies admittedly have one aim in common, each one of them wants to make people happy, open the door, and show the way to fulfillment. Certainly this is the motive behind socialism. Karl Marx was moved with compassion as he watched the miserable conditions under which the working class of his day had to live and to suffer; and his plan and program aimed at new happiness for them. Nobody can deny that his influence brought about a great deal of progress that scarcely would have been made without his influence. Yet the question remains: Can and will his system really bring ultimate fulfillment to the needs of man? In these days of utmost prosperity in my own country, we can see how unhappy people can be even with all their wishes and desires fulfilled and amply satisfied. Nevertheless, a vacuum arises, and that is what we call "nihilism." There is everything and yet there is nothing. What is life for? The answer: Life is nothing! Keep it or throw it away, just as you like; real happiness, genuine fulfillment, stays out of your reach. Nothingness is all you can achieve and find. Is there any answer at all? We may bypass here all other philosophies and religions. For ultimately, they all culminate in Buddhism, which makes of need a virtue and of nothingness a desirable aim, and this is what man alone, the human being, may make of his own existence.

Christ Jesus shows us a different way when we pass through the door that he has opened before us. It is the way of "reconciliation." In his witness to this action and performance of his Lord, the apostle Paul recognizes the decisive event that gives the true answer to the tormenting problem of human life and its meaning: What is life for? Life is not meaningless and not in vain. "By him all things consist," and he, Jesus the Christ, has reconciled you—"to

present you holy and unblamable and unreprovable in his
sight." Reconciliation points out that man is not left to
himself, and life's fulfillment cannot be found or achieved
in individual solitude and preoccupation with self. That
has become man's basic error, his original sin, that he de-
cided to live and care for himself; and surely this has
become, if ever it has been otherwise, the common, the
universal characteristic, and simultaneously, the dividing
and conflict-producing element in the nature of the human
race, of the whole human generation. If anyone could
and would do away with this fatal trait of man, which,
universal as it is, of necessity generates universal inhumanity, he would be the One whom all the world should
follow and obey. This has been done in the One who is the
"Christ for the World"!

For nearly two thousand years the Christian message has
proclaimed Jesus as this longed-for liberator and restorer
of humanity. He is the one who in his earthly days with-
stood all temptation of love of self and thus refused to
become inhuman. He won his disciples over by his truly
brotherly and human concern for them so that they accepted the personal relationship that he offered. As they
received his Spirit, their natural inhumanity and self-
concern changed to trust in his Father, whom they now
accepted as their own Father. It changed to concern, love,
obedience, and solidarity with their fellow beings. There,
for them, was the answer to the question: What is life
for?

We call it "faith." And this "faith" in itself is universal in
character; this faith accepts the command of its Lord,
without any scruple or hesitation, to go into all the world
and preach the gospel, the glad tidings, to every creature.
For this person, Jesus the Christ, has become and is the

center of God's creation. Nobody can live and nothing can exist except by him, who gives and who is the answer. This gives meaning to the existence and to the continuance of God's world. That is both the background and wellspring of the apostle's praise of his Lord's absolute and living majesty: "By him were all things created," and "for him," and "he is before all things, and by him all things consist." God himself is working in him, "for it pleased the Father that in him should all fulness dwell" and "by him to reconcile all things unto himself." Only to us it seems surprising that these eleven disciples, some uneducated fishermen, and others of no special reputation, began to face the whole world; to the disciples it was different: Christ for the World! They knew this really was their Lord's commission and they were convinced that their mandate was meant for and needed by all, and they knew we owe it to all!

The Christian church does her mission work because it belongs to us all. We cannot help taking it on as our own responsibility, once we have come to know that the gospel is not just our personal religion or philosophy of life, but that it is immensely more. It is the one way behind the open door that leads to life's fulfillment for those who find this way and walk it, in the footsteps of Him who calls us, who calls everybody: "I am the way, the truth, and the life"!

We owe it to the whole world. We must not shut our eyes, either to the neediness of those who live far away or to them who live about us but who do not know what the gospel is, and there are many, many. The world shares in a common sense of apprehension and fear that inhumanity will be victorious and destroy God's world. We have God's offer that will rescue and give us new life. It is he who liberates us from love of self and transforms it to love of God and love of our neighbor. This is the answer to the question: What is life for? "Christ for the World"!

DR. BLAKE CONTINUED

It was Wendell Lewis Willkie in the early 1940's who, by his exuberant speeches and through a widely read little book entitled *One World,* made an end to the once popular isolationism of the thinking of many North Americans.

Someone said shortly after: "Now at last the United States Department of State is catching up to an understanding of the world that has long been taken for granted by the women's missionary societies of our churches!"

It is not by chance that it is missionary-minded Christians in all the Western nations who are still among the "advanced" thinkers and who were among the first to realize that old ways of thought about the world had been made obsolete by the events of the twentieth century. The connection is that those involved in Christian missionary activity, whether in the first century, the sixteenth, or the nineteenth century, were forced by their missionary activity to reflect upon the New Testament basis and authority for it. The passages most often quoted even yet for this would be Matt. 28:19–20: "Go therefore and make disciples of all nations, baptizing them in the name of the Father and of the Son and of the Holy Spirit, teaching them to observe all that I have commanded you; and lo, I am with you always, to the close of the age"; and Acts 1:8: "But you shall receive power when the Holy Spirit has come upon you; and you shall be my witnesses in Jerusalem and in all Judea and Samaria and to the end of the earth"; and Mark 16:15 (even though the authenticity of the text is doubtful): "Go into all the world and preach the gospel to the whole creation."

But as we speak to you here in Philadelphia on the theme "Christ for the World," it may surprise some of the more missionary-minded among you that we chose this Colossians passage upon which to base our dialogue.

Some critics of the ecumenical movement charge it with being really unconcerned about "foreign missions" in the traditional sense. That is a profound misunderstanding of the ecumenical movement, for at its base is not only the old urgency to preach the gospel to every creature in every nation, but there is added a profound theological urgency that was sometimes missing in the past—an urgency that is most clearly expressed in these verses that have been read from the first chapter of the letter to the Colossians. Let me remind you what the apostle says here.

He is writing to a people who have been newly converted to Jesus Christ. They had heard the preaching and they had responded. In the verses just before the passage read, he reminded the new Christians in Colossae that God "has delivered us from the dominion of darkness and transferred us to the kingdom of his beloved Son." Note that the apostle includes himself with these very newest converts. God has delivered not you, *us*, and God "has transferred *us* to the kingdom of his Son." If there was a weakness in the traditional missionary movement, it centered on a universal sinful tendency, which the great missionary apostle here avoids, of making the missionary himself the benefactor of the converted people rather than God through Jesus Christ being fully exalted as the sole benefactor by his overwhelming grace both to preacher and to convert. In the great modern missionary century, the nineteenth, it may not have been quite so crucial as it is obvious now in our half of the twentieth century, to be quite sure that wherever it is, Christian preaching avoid the sin of pride of possession, the owning of the gospel.

It is hard enough in our day to know how to give foreign aid without patronage even when people are starving for food and are economically prostrate. How do you do it? The dignity of hungry men, we are beginning slowly to understand, must be respected even in that kind of situation; and Jesus Christ himself cannot be exported like a CARE package out of an affluent generosity or the spirit of such generosity.

Before the two great wars of our time, the peoples of Asia, Africa, and Latin America were willing to receive both spiritual and material gifts from the West, which implied that they needed what we had. Today Jesus Christ will be received by these other peoples only as we make it explicitly clear that we understand full well that we need him as desperately as our Savior as they need him as theirs.

The passage itself begins, as Dr. Niemöller has said, by exalting Jesus Christ in limitless cosmic terms as the revelation of the invisible God, as the preexistent creator of all things spiritual and material, and as the one organizing and cohering power of all reality. The passage then proceeds through Christ to exalt Christ's church, his body, and to do it in terms that should prostrate every Christian in holy awe. Next we are reminded that the fullness of God dwelt in Jesus, especially as he died on the cross—his moment of abasement being the moment of his victory— thus and only thus providing reconciliation and peace to God's whole wide world.

The missionary movement can move forward in power in our time only as Christians continue in this old and saving faith, never shifting from this one hope of salvation in Jesus Christ and in him alone.

In January of this year, Dr. Niemöller and I were in

Eastern Nigeria together not far from that Calabar where that great Scots-woman missionary, Mary Slessor, gave her life to Christ and for him to God's people in Africa a century ago. How moving and romantic are the stories of those great heroes for Christ, men and women who were the missionary pioneers in the wooded jungles of equatorial Africa! They gave themselves, their health, their lives for Christ and in his love to strange peoples "hostile in mind, doing evil deeds," to refer again to our passage. They were murdered, some of them; they were stricken with malaria, for which there was then no cure or hindrance; they left behind them their homes and hearths and loved ones; they embraced instead loneliness, spiritual and physical—all this they did in faith, going out "to a place" that they "were to receive as an inheritance"—"not knowing where" they were to go, by faith sojourning "in the land of promise, as in a foreign land."

But Eastern Nigeria is no longer a "foreign land" to the Christian, to those who go in the name of the same Jesus Christ today. A Christian will be received hospitably by the distinguished Christian governor of Eastern Nigeria, a product of the mission of Mary Slessor and her fellow Scots. The prime minister of Eastern Nigeria will be worshiping with you in one of Enugu's Methodist churches, if you should happen to follow John Wesley's tradition and go there with him. The high judge, should you stand before him in court or call upon him at his home, is an Anglican, a product of the fruitful sacrifices of England's Church Missionary Society.

But not for very long will you identify these Christians in Nigeria by the land or the mission from which those first missionaries came. This year those three churches are uniting into a single church of Nigeria, no longer guided in their life nor restrained from their own decisions by

European or American churches or traditions—guided and constrained, rather, by the same Jesus Christ who called the first missionaries from the West and from the North to go to that tropic land.

And now as these Nigerian men and women stand themselves responsible before God for the continuing mission in their land and on their continent, some Christians in Britain, the continent of Europe, and in North America find it very hard to adjust to this new situation. Is there a place any longer, they ask, for white missionaries in Africa or Asia? Yes, there is a place, but it is not the old place. It is a new place that somehow doesn't seem quite so romantic. And the requirements are more stringent than they were before.

For example, no suburban church in Philadelphia, or center city either, can produce an acceptable Christian missionary today for Nigeria, except by way of full involvement in the black center of this very city. Only as we realize that we too live in a mission field, a field of desperate and crying need for Jesus Christ, dare we volunteer to witness for him in Africa today.

But the old great urge and the old romance seem gone to many. At last Paul's hyperbole in Col. 1:23 seems to have been fulfilled: "The gospel," he wrote, "which you heard, . . . has been preached to every creature under heaven." It wasn't true quite literally then, nor is it now, but at least now there are no new rivers to explore, no new jungles, except here and there in the remotest Andes or Himalayas, or in the highlands of Central Congo. But does this really mean that the great missionary day is ended? Does this mean that high purpose, and great dedication, and full self-sacrifice are no longer needed?

No, the mission exists, a thrilling mission, and it is on six continents, not three. The foreigner (the stranger, the

alien, and the estranged) can be found five hundred yards
from this church in which we worship—no need to travel
five thousand miles. There will be no less travel in the
cause of Christ, but some of it will be coming in other
directions. Nigerians will come to help their fellow Christians preach and live the gospel, both in Philadelphia, Mississippi, and in Philadelphia, Pennsylvania. And all danger,
I remind you, has not gone. Last year it was more dangerous to preach or to witness for Jesus Christ in Mississippi, and last week for one Christian missionary in
Alabama, than in most parts of Africa.

But neither the risk of danger nor the excitement of
travel to far or strange places was ever the essential motivation of the foreign missionary movement, nor the source
of its true romance or its deepest drama. The exaltation
of the mission has ever come from the exaltation of the
one Lord Jesus Christ.

Today, it is true that the patterns of mission are not
always quite so clear as they seemed to be to our grand-
fathers. But the call comes as clear and it comes from the
same Jesus Christ. And his call is being heard above the
strident clamor of selfishness and over the dull stagnation
of material comfort by those who have ears to hear. But
the call is being heard by those alone who "continue in the
faith, stable and steadfast." Yes, by those "not shifting
from the hope of the gospel" which they themselves had
earlier heard.

And who is it that calls us? Jesus Christ, "the image of
the invisible God, the first-born of all creation; . . . the
head of the body, the church. . . . In him all the fulness of
God was pleased to dwell." Even Jesus Christ, by whom
alone all things can be reconciled "whether on earth or in
heaven, making peace by the blood of his cross."

THE DIALOGUE

As Dr. Blake finished his sermon and took his place at the table next to Dr. Niemöller, the German churchman lost no time in commenting:

"My perception of what you, Gene, have just told us about mission work means something very new, at least to some of us. To others it is a reminder of changes that we have known now for a number of years but that we no longer take into account. We may indeed get missionaries from foreign countries and nations, and that reminds me of the Third World Conference of Christian Youth in Kottayam in 1952, when M. M. Thomas asked me when he said good-by: 'When shall we have to send missionaries to your country?' At first I was really very much taken aback—but then it dawned on me that we should indeed ask our friends of those former 'foreign mission countries' to visit us as witnesses to the Lord in their faith."

"This of course has been happening," Dr. Blake said. "Some of it quite personal and some of it quite official and programmed in all directions over some years now. But still, most of us Americans, and I would guess most Germans, don't think it is necessary. That is to say, within the church! After all, we think of ourselves as having the gospel, and why would anyone need to bring it from Africa? I remind you, and us all of course, that we don't own this gospel! I think we need somehow to get this across to Asians and Africans and Latin Americans. Jesus himself lived in Palestine in the Middle East and not in a part of the world of our ancestors. Culturally, Jesus is in many ways stranger to the United States than to Ethiopia, a part of Africa. But we have enmeshed Jesus Christ with our culture, with the result that many people both in our own culture and elsewhere in the world do not really see him as what we have always professed him to be—the Savior of the world!"

Dr. Blake then asked this question: "Martin, is 'nihilism,' as you spoke about it, basically taking the place of either the old Christian faith or the adherence to the secular hope of socialism and Communism in your land and in Western Europe?"

Dr. Niemöller's answer came thoughtfully. "When I spoke of 'nihilism,' I thought of those many, many people nowadays who really are longing for Christ without being aware of it. For nihilism has taken a hold on them, and they no longer know what life is for, man's life in this world. I believe that here we have a very real challenge to our missionary outreach in our own countries. People who have no answer to the question, What is my life for? come to church not because they are Christians but because they remember, and are being reminded, that the church professes to have the answer to this question of what man's life is for, for what purpose God created man! He created man to be his child and his fellowman's brother. I am always quite glad when I meet people who are now facing the real question after they have lost faith in their own strength and vain hopes."

Dr. Blake proceeded in a somewhat lighter vein. He said: "I am reminded of Lord Fisher, the former Archbishop of Canterbury, whom you know very well. He was in this country not too long ago and was being pressed by reporters, as sometimes foreign dignitaries are, as he was saying some good things about the church in Britain. One of the reporters said, 'But your churches are empty; how do you explain that as compared to our American churches?' And the Archbishop, with his usual wit, said,

'Well, the only trouble is, you are fifty years behind the times!' "

"Is this true?" Dr. Blake continued. "This is the real question that we are beginning to face in this country. Theologically we have been 'fifty years behind the times.' " Grinning broadly, he said: "We have to wait until your German theological books are translated before we get a chance to read them and catch up with the latest school in German theology. But the fact is that we are different here—and yet so much the same. You spoke about the reason that communism doesn't have much of a chance among us. I think that is true because it is too absolute. How do we avoid what American society gives primary emphasis—not the pluralism of our society (we have been a pluralistic society from the beginning), but the tendency toward syncretism; that is to say, the attitude imposed on all of us by the modern world. 'Oh, we are all going to the same place, and whoever has any faith, no matter in whom or what, this is a good thing, and after all, people need it to keep them quiet.' What do we do, how do we break through this in our time?"

Dr. Niemöller spoke gravely: "Do we really know the difference and the superiority of the authority of Christ Jesus over and against claims by this or that competing person or this or that competing *Weltanschauung* or religion?"

"May I interrupt," Dr. Blake cut in, "simply to say that the first point you made of relativism means, 'Ours isn't best either, but it is the one that I happen to like.' There is no absoluteness, as you said. This is what is bothering me. I can argue about Jesus Christ as against Buddhism or heathenism or whatever 'ism.' But how do we break through the idea that 'after all, it's human to respect other peoples' points of view' no matter whether they are true or not?"

"Yes," Dr. Niemöller answered, "I believe that it is not enough merely to say, 'This is my conviction and my experience.' We should induce others, not to syncretism, but to make the experiment. There is no other way to show them that they are not as happy, for instance, as Marx wanted them to be or as any *Weltanschauung* or religion wants to make them, and to explain to them that here is really Somebody who is the Way. Paul says it in his letter to the Galatians: 'before whose eyes Jesus Christ hath been evidently set forth, crucified among you.'"

"I think we just have to show the picture," Dr. Niemöller continued, "and in preaching give an impression of this human, really human, being who becomes our brother and thereby creates a kind of response; not necessarily from our side, not necessarily in itself. It is the Holy Spirit at work who will create faith."

Dr. Blake concluded the discussion: "Martin, yesterday when I was questioning you about truth and the ecumenical movement, you said that sometimes understanding is not so important as the actual personal faith; you referred to the concentration camp. There is an interesting novel, the Romanian novel *Incognito*. I recommend it to people who want to see one way (not necessarily a Christian way) in which one modern man is struggling, not intellectually but practically, to move out of the ideology of communism that he has rejected, even though he once was a Communist. He has rejected all faith, all religion, all theology, but somehow he is beginning to act in love, just in love, no matter what! Though he may not put a name to this love, he is seeking God. We Christians need to read such novels to see how great is our problem of communicating the gospel to men in the modern world."

CHAPTER THREE

POLITICS AND ECONOMICS UNDER THE LORD JESUS CHRIST

_____

TEXT: I CORINTHIANS 10:23 to 11:1
Wednesday, March 17

DR. BLAKE BEGAN

There are certain myths currently popular in our country which make it excessively difficult even to begin a discussion of politics or economics and their relationship either to the Lord Jesus Christ or to his church.

The first such myth is that some of the peoples of the world are peace-loving and others are warmongers. Some nations are the good people and the others are the bad people, as in a TV Western. The reason that I say this is a myth is that experience shows that to categorize nations in this fashion has, in fact, no objective reality. During the third of a century that I have been a Presbyterian minister, Germany was bad, according to the myth, from 1932 to 1946, and since that time it has been good, according to the myth. From 1932 to 1942, the U.S.S.R. was bad. Then for six years, from 1942 to 1948, the U.S.S.R. was very, very bad, and since 1961 it has been bad, but not so bad as China, which had always been good until 1948, since which date it has been increasingly bad.

From 1940 to 1946, Japan was very bad. Since 1946, Japan is very, very good. Spain was good from 1932 to 1936, then until 1939 a mixture, and then fifteen years bad, and for the last ten years or so, good. Nigeria and the Cameroun are good. Sudan, Ghana, and Guinea are bad. So it goes—the myth. Even without a change of government, or even change of policy, nations, however, change from good to bad, very much as in a poorly scripted TV Western, where the characters in the last scenes have no relationship to what they were in the first scenes that the director shot.

In the economic field, the myths are almost as confusing. There are some among us who promote the myth that interference by the Federal Government in business is always bad, this despite federal protective tariffs, federal laws on monetary and immigration control based upon the sufficient availability of cheap labor and cheap money, which some of the very same people continue to support as a federal action. At the other extreme in the political spectrum of our society are "doctrinaire liberals," who promote the myth that federal planning and control of economic life is always good and necessary to solve any problem even though the side effects of such planning and control often tend to destroy the very economic freedom to which they are fully committed. Such myths blind us to the realities that we face.

And there are two realities toward which all of us ought to turn our attention as Christians, which cut across these blinding, confusing myths to which men hold so emotionally.

The first one of these is that there is a life and death struggle, a power struggle, going on in our world between atheistic communism and the traditional Western nations, which once could be called Christendom. The struggle is as to which will survive as the organizing force in the one interdependent world clearly coming. I mention this reality first because many critics of the ecumenical movement, for which Dr. Niemöller and I stand, have charged us and all the other ecumenical Christian leaders with being the tools or the dupes of international communism, when, on the contrary, it is my conviction that the position that has been taken by the ecumenical movement and its leaders is the only hope the world has of burying the communist ideology, and that is by giving to the peoples of all the world a live alternative to the Marxist, Leninist, Stalinist, and Chinese deathtrap into which the underdeveloped nations of Asia, Africa, and Latin America seem to be plunging. And the burden of this message is that the West will lose this contest with communism unless we find the way truly to exalt Jesus Christ as the Lord of love and freedom rather than to continue to fight communism by the myths of the "good guys" and the "bad guys," about which I have already spoken.

The other reality that this generation must face intelligently and morally is the technological revolution that is, in fact, changing both East and West at a speed with which neither Western nor communist ideologists are able to cope. The fact is that the new productive capacity made possible by automated factories can, on the one hand, do away with the poverty that has always been the greatest burden of man but, at the same time, threatens to lay a greater burden on human beings spiritually than poverty and scarcity ever did.

The visible symbol of all this is the high-rise, low-cost, apartment buildings that mark and mar the skylines of every major city in the world. You see them in Moscow, in

Paris, and in New York. We accept them because they are clearly better than the five-story walk-up tenements they are designed to replace. But we hardly have begun to subject the modern urban life that the new technology is forcing upon us, both East and West, to any moral scrutiny as to what human life will be like when we have reached the end of the road down which the whole world is now blindly rushing as it is pushed by its automated machine. There is no dearth of prophets of doom like George Orwell, who wrote his *1984*, but so far there is almost a complete lack of creative prophets who will guide us to economic and political decisions that will in fact preserve human dignity and human freedom and man himself from the destruction toward which he appears to be heading.

It is against the background of this very brief analysis of our economic and political dilemma that in these few minutes I must try to proclaim the relevance of the Lord Jesus Christ. If Jesus Christ is in fact our Lord, and we are not willing to limit his Lordship to a kind of individual morality that was relevant to an agricultural society of scarcity, there are at least four Christian and Biblical convictions that must underlie, and ultimately determine, all our political and economic views as Christians.

The first is the proclamation of the psalmist that sums up the Biblical premise upon which Christian faith rests: "The earth is the Lord's, and the fulness thereof; the world, and they that dwell therein." There are two convictions expressed in that verse which we who profess Christian faith in this affluent land are in deepest danger of either forgetting, or worse, repudiating. God, the creator and sovereign, made and owns and rules the whole earth. Its riches belong to him—not to us. We are his creatures. He is our creator. Here is the most fundamental difference between communist atheism and Christian faith, but it is also the most fundamental difference between Christian faith and Western materialism. Man's control and exploitation of the good earth from Genesis to Revelation is subjected in the Biblical view to the transcendent and sovereign God to whom man as God's creature owes full obedience.

The other Christian conviction, expressed in that one verse, is that of the universality of this transcendent God's concern. Not only is God sovereign of the whole earth and its riches, he is also Lord of all men in every land and nation. Here too is the sharp contrast between Christian faith and the doctrinaire atheism of Marxism and the practical atheism of much of what once was Christendom. All men are God's creatures and his potential sons. It was for all men, of every race and people, of every nation and of every clime that God did send his Son to die upon a cross. He died for rich and poor, for hater and the hated, for saints and sinners, for the cultured and the uncultured, even for those whose mother tongue is not English, Martin!

Second, the meek "shall inherit the earth." This Beatitude of our Lord is almost more embarrassing to us Americans than the one we shall be discussing on Friday, "Blessed are you poor, for yours is the kingdom of God." A week ago last Sunday night there was shown on the news a set of television pictures of the march in Selma, Alabama, which showed Dr. Martin Luther King's supporters being brutally beaten by representatives of the state and local government. It is to such pictures that non-Christians and half Christians point when they resist this understanding of Christian faith that I am now proclaiming. They say: "The meek 'shall inherit the earth.' Ha! How can you repeat with a straight face such foolishness when the meek are beaten with clubs and kicked as they lie helpless upon the very earth you Christians say the meek shall inherit?"

But I remind you that it was just such television pictures shown in May of 1963 (of police dogs and the fire hoses) that began the process which in these next months will overthrow the political power of the Governor Wallaces and the Sheriff Clarks who do seem for a time to rule the earth. Our Christian faith holds that "God is not mocked," neither is his hand "shortened, that it cannot save, or his ear dull, that it cannot hear."

Third, "Man shall not live by bread alone." These words of Jesus addressed, you remember, to the tempter himself, are a clear expression of our Christian conviction that men are more than smart animals, that within every man is a longing and a potential for communion with God, in whose image he has been made. But the world is in a cynical mood on this subject in both communist and noncommunist lands. Popular "realism" in both East and West is willing to treat men simply as "mouths" and "hands" as if man's function was simply to work and to survive. But the spirit of man is not a mere figment of imagination. Man's spirit is as real as man's body. Man is capable of love that is not merely an extension of his sexual instinct for survival. Man is capable of self-sacrifice that is not merely an exponent of masochism. Man can make beauty and man can respond to the beauty that God and other men have made. By God's grace, man can repent of evil and turn to good, and he can discipline himself and find his joy in human and humane community instead of being driven by his natural selfish desires. It is our faith that "man shall not live by bread alone."

Finally, I quote the apostle Paul as he reached his climax in the Scripture lesson that you have just heard, when he wrote: "So whether you eat or drink, or whatever you do, do all to the glory of God." Again there are two aspects of this apostolic exhortation to Christians that I wish to apply to the subject of our discussion this evening. Note that the apostle understands clearly that all Christians, even in one church, cannot be expected to agree upon the concrete moral application of Christianity even on such simple questions as dietary laws and practices. How much less likely is it that any congregation of Christians could be expected to agree on a single Christian line on either politics or economics in the twentieth century.

But here in this verse and in this passage the apostle makes it equally clear that Christian faith and obedience demand that we be involved in all the moral decisions of life, and that whatever we do, we offer up what we do to the praise and the glory of God himself. The essential problem of the churches in Philadelphia, in America, and in all Christendom today is not caused by our political and economic differences of conviction. The essential problem is that few of us on any side are clearly willing to recognize Jesus Christ as Lord even of our economics and politics. Let us press forward then as Christians into increasing involvement in the world as servants of the Lord Jesus Christ, giving praise to the God of all history and in faith that he will use our service if we offer it unto him and will rule and overrule our acts. And to his name be the glory and the praise.

DR. NIEMÖLLER CONTINUED

In the New Testament we find no reference to the stand Christians ought to take in politics and economics except for a few very general remarks and directives on behavior over against the secular authorities. We think, for instance, of Jesus' instructions for those who ask him: "Is it lawful to give tribute unto Caesar, or not?" or we think of Paul's warning against insurrection: "Let every soul be subject unto the higher powers." This seems to signify, more or less, that the church, the Christian community as the company of Christ's followers, should not be concerned with worldly affairs at all. The text we have heard is part of a discussion about Christians in Corinth who participated in pagan meals and ate meat of pagan sacrifices; thus far, there is hardly a relation to our topic and the issue with which we want to deal. A similar reflection can be made on Christian behavior and participation in economics.

All that we find in the New Testament on these spheres of human life and activities seems to be Jesus' call to faithfulness and charity when he blames the "evil servant," who, in forgetting his Lord's coming, begins to treat his fellows badly, and when Jesus sharply criticizes the "unjust steward," who wasted his Lord's goods. Wherever the problems of politics and economics turn up among the disciples of Christ, the church, there the members will find advice and instruction how to respond, namely, in accordance with the spirit of that person, whom they know as Lord and whom they are called upon—we are called upon —to follow in all things. As long as Christian people can obey the orders of a "higher power" without dissociating themselves from their highest and ultimate authority, the Lord Jesus Christ, they can, and even must, pay "tribute unto Caesar." As long as they can take their place in any economic structure without ignoring their obligation to their neighbor, their fellow beings, they may and also must do so. This is to say that Christians cannot leave the realm of Christ's dominion and rule even in politics and in economics.

When faced with the issues of secular authority that would entail disobedience toward Christ, we have to prefer being disobedient to the worldly power, lest we should deny him who is "Lord of all." One must obey God rather than man. In my country, we had to take our stand in this in no uncertain terms when Adolf Hitler became the legal authority and issued laws and orders that were clearly contradictory to the commandments and to the Spirit of Jesus Christ. There was no alternative. We had to disobey irrespective of those consequences which we knew might, and indeed did, follow.

For us today, and for some generations before us, the problem of the Christian's attitude and his relation to politics as well as economics basically has changed. In the times of the New Testament, the Christians were passive objects of what happened in politics. They could not help having to accept the conditions of economic life as they were; the status of the constituency of the church was such that they—slaves, handymen, workmen, and craftsmen—really could not have, and had not, any influence on politics or on economic life. This has greatly changed in our world with its Christian tradition and democratic structure. Yet, for a long time the churches have refused to take notice of this change and have clung to the old tradition. We teach our people how to live as Christians in the political and the economic world in which we find ourselves. There has been—and still is—an even more definite disengagement from politics and economics in the Christian camp. This has developed especially in the regions of former state churches, where the church is understood as an institution that merely serves the religious life of the population. The political, economic, social, educational, and all other parts of human and social life have their own structure and their own system of laws and rules.

Here, then, the Christian task is restricted to the religious sphere only, and this has proved to be clashing. Christian people in Hitler's Germany who were engaged in political work with the Nazis, under their laws and rules of political life, and who had not been forewarned by the church, became the indictors in this clash. They accused us, the church, that we had not told them in time what they were really getting into and what they would be up against. Christians must know that all human life, all activities, be it in politics, economics, social developments, in science and scholarship, even in arts and literature, have to be focused on service for other human beings. This alone is Christian by ethical standards. We cannot refrain from using our influence as Christian citizens to help create such conditions in politics and economics as will best serve human needs and interests.

And this certainly means a break, a definite breach of what people generally understand by religion; Christianity is no religion in that sense, for there is no relationship to God and no connection between God and man when he passes by his fellow. The firstborn claims: "No man cometh unto the Father, but by me." This is the religious part of Christianity. When the Lord states, "Inasmuch as ye have done it unto one of the least of these my brethren, ye have done it unto me," this then is the ethical side of Christianity. These two parts are inseparable; they are one—to love God and to love your neighbor. Therefore, man, the human being, sets the standard of all human action and authority in this world, for in the whole creation, according to the Christian message, God cares for nothing and for nobody more than for his children on earth. He created them in his own image and he pays the whole price to redeem them. He wants them to love their Creator and Father and to love their fellows, whom he, the Father, loves. Consequently the church knows no higher value in the whole realm of creation than man, the human being. The non-Christian may have a different scale of values. He may have his own ideal, for which to live and to die he thinks is right and for which he may use even his human fellows as means, as instruments, in order to accomplish his most desirable aim. The Christian in the Christian community, the church, is not allowed this kind of idealism. We know no ideal of greater importance and value in the sight of our heavenly Father than our human brother and sister, our fellow being, for whom Christ Jesus died, for whom God gave himself. If we agree that as Christians we cannot do otherwise—and all Christianity ought to agree to this valuation of man—then we must use our civic rights and all political influence at our command for the making of such politics as will serve man, so that he may lead his life as a child of God and as a fellow of his brother. For thousands of years, politics has purposed dominion, influence, authority, and power. Politics under the Lord Jesus Christ ought to take aim at serving man and renounce exploiting him for other ends.

Therefore, I am sure that the World Council of Churches chose the right way when it promoted and advocated human rights and religious liberty; warned of nuclear means of mass destruction and of warfare as a means of politics; recommended and asked for negotiation in all cases of controversy; condemned all kinds of race discrimination; and became and remained a genuine friend, adviser, and promoter of the United Nations organization and its work. Politics, in Christian interpretation, has to serve man and not help any special group to profit at the expense of others. It is meant to contribute to the fulfillment of God's will and plan: "Behold, how good and how pleasant it is for brethren to dwell together in unity"! There is no special directive in the New Testament how politics should be geared so that it might become "politics under the Lord Jesus Christ," but he is Lord of all, and his Lordship must be recognized. His Spirit must permeate all sorts of human interrelations to which we Christians, we the church, may contribute. Paul tells us: "Give none offense, neither to the Jews, nor to the Gentiles, . . . seeking . . . the profit of many, that they may be saved"! Surely politics means an important commission and mission for the whole church of Christ Jesus, not to be overlooked or neglected, but to be acknowledged and begun!

When it comes to economics, we Christians think and work, knowing that by faith we no longer need to care for ourselves: "Casting all your care upon him, for he careth for you"! Redeemed from ourselves by faith, as we are, we are free to serve our neighbor as we follow the apostle's call: "Let no man seek his own, but every man another's wealth." We all know that many hundred millions of human brothers suffer from malnutrition and that day by day one hundred thousand human beings die from starvation, while the Christian world abounds in riches. Mankind, again, does not visualize the value that God places upon his human creature. We preach the gospel as we point to man's obligation to God to use all economic possibilities and achievements for that service which humanity demands; for what humanity demands, God the Father of Christ Jesus demands. The ecumenical movement's "Life and Work" program, which was begun forty years ago, has continuously stressed this very point and has produced and developed a great deal of economic aid; but most important is that now this problem of economics has become an international and universal concern. The World Council of Churches will encourage and assist all efforts to overcome a disgraceful state of affairs, which is inhuman and therefore unchristian.

We conclude: The Christian churches cannot remain aloof from any area of the society of man, as the general trend of thought of bygone days would have it, merely because the New Testament does not afford direct instructions. The question remains: Is such practiced disengagement in conformity with our Lord's will and Spirit? Most assuredly, wherever we see human beings threatened into becoming pawns, the church of Christ must take their part, must try to help them—these human beings for whom Christ died. The church of Christ must care because politics and economics have to do with people. The church of Christ must ensure that politics and economics serve people and not that people become means to an end for politics and economics!

THE DIALOGUE

Those were two powerful sermons. Again, as on Monday and Tuesday, there prevailed throughout the church a breathless quiet, which happens only when people are really touched and listen attentively. Dr. Blake had a smile on his face when he said:

"Martin, I am going to ask you a question that you would not volunteer, I am sure. That is the reason I am asking it. What does the position of the United States in international affairs today look like to a European Christian? That is a mean question, I know, but I think it is the most important thing that you can say to Christians here in Philadelphia and in our country as well."

Dr. Niemöller, always willing to give his personal opinions and viewpoints, employs restraint when it comes to judgment in general terms. He said, "I think there is no general consent in Europe today on how people judge the attitude, activities, and politics of the United States; but let me ask you contrariwise, Gene, which special part of the politics of the United States do you have in mind?"

"I am thinking of our position in international affairs," Dr. Blake said. "You can talk about Vietnam if you want, our position confronting the Soviet Union, or the mainland of China, any part of that, including our use of atomic energy, our use of our wealth. I want you to level with us!"

"Well, then," Dr. Niemöller began, "I shall say first of all that I regret very much that America is, as it looks to me, and I think to many people in the world, still very much preoccupied with the idea of power politics and influential politics, and that it is not taking into consideration, in a Christian way, the fate of human beings.

"As to Vietnam, another question arises, and I think it is spreading not only in Asia but also in Africa: The politics of the United States is interpreted as neocolonialism, as you deal with areas and with people in those areas who are not really a concern or a task for the United States. Also, I think that the most recent past in your country has added a great deal to this kind of mistrust. People will say, 'Why are they trying, even pretending, to look after the freedom of people in Asia as long as their own people in their own country have to fight for their freedom, for their human rights, their civil rights, and things like that?' This reaction, if not judgment, on the part of people in the world, would be much alleviated if you succeeded in solving first your problem of racial discrimination and differentiation in civil rights in your own country."

Dr. Blake persisted: "Is our unpopularity across the world—our Information Services seem to be now the first target for rocks in many lands!—is this unpopularity inevitable for a nation that has as much political power as we have today, or is it perhaps because somehow none of us has been able to rise to the interdependence of a single world? What I am really getting at is this, how much of this use of power politics is inevitable as there is order, order of sorts, to be kept? The Soviet Union exercises it over a good deal of the world. They are not always popular in Romania and Hungary either. Is it because we are trying to dominate with politics, as you suggested, or is it because none of us yet sees the solution of living in peace, except that we are frightened to start a war which may, as the modern term is, escalate into an atomic explosion?"

"It is quite possible," Dr. Niemöller answered, "that this temptation cannot be avoided altogether. I would outline as your country's main task in politics to convince people —those concerned as well as the onlookers—that politics is being made for the best of the human beings in those areas in which the United States is active. And there is the question!"

"Let me ask one more question, Martin," Dr. Blake said. "In Portland, Oregon, a few weeks ago, you said something that was a bit of a shock to me. I think maybe it has to do with your own country rather than this country. Did I understand you correctly when you suggested that even if the Soviet Union and the United States now withdrew their influence in Germany, Germany still would be divided? And if so, what did you mean by that?"

"Yes," Dr. Niemöller replied, "I am quite convinced of

what I said, and I really meant it. Ever since 1949 we have
lived in two Germanys and have been led to live in different directions. It is much more difficult to imagine a reunification of the two Germanys of today than it would
have been in 1950 or 1952. For the time being, I see no
possibility of a genuine reunification, meaning one state
with one economy and one kind of politics. Prerequisites
are, for instance, whether America and Russia will come to
terms on the political level, as I hope! Also, on the political
level, whether Western and Eastern Germany will begin
to speak to each other, which now they don't. At present,
the situation is hopeless as far as economics and the social
structure are concerned, because in Western Germany we
live in a free economy; and the great majority of the people
in Eastern Germany do not want the return of the owners
of the big estates in Pomerania and Brandenburg, and so
on. The industrial workers in Saxony certainly don't want
to see the industrial world of Saxony handed back to private capital. They have become accustomed to the thought
of being the owners of the country even if this is true only
in an idealistic sort of way. They do not work less now than
formerly, under the owners of those big estates, but they
are aware of the fact that they no longer labor for the
profit of one man who does nothing but reap the fruit of
their labor. This is definitely a thing of the past. On my
trips through Eastern Germany I have not yet found anybody, no rural workers in the northern part either, who
wants to have the former conditions back.

"This is equally true of Russia. I have not spoken to any
man who favors the former life under the czars. One has
to keep in mind, however, that the number of people who
still remember life under the czars is now decreasing
rather fast.

"The situation in Saxony is similar to that. In addition, there is a considerable amount of pride among the people in Eastern Germany. They have rebuilt as much as they could from complete destruction. They had to pay reparations, and the Russians removed everything from the country that seemed still of use to them. There was no capital, no loans, no foreign aid, to help rebuild the industry. Accordingly, the labor group in this part of Eastern Germany is especially proud of their achievements. 'Nobody helped us, and today we are second only to the Soviet Union in industrial production and volume of output.' "

Dr. Blake expressed appreciation to Dr. Niemöller and commented: "My main reason for asking these questions of Dr. Niemöller was that he is one of the few people in Europe who can be counted on not necessarily to say the expected thing, the popular thing—not even in his own country. But he can always be expected to gear his opinions in terms of his faith in Jesus Christ.

"Of this we need more in our discussions in this country —and the world over!"

CHAPTER FOUR

MANY PEOPLES AND RACES—
YET ONE FAMILY

TEXT: EPHESIANS 3:14–21; ACTS 10:1–46
Thursday, March 18

DR. NIEMÖLLER BEGAN

The Lord Jesus Christ is Lord of all. We thought about this yesterday when dealing with "Politics and Economics Under the Lord Jesus Christ." The same truth is before us today, as Paul in the epistle to the Ephesians reminds us in what is also a prayer of intercession. It is a prayer of adoration, glorifying the Father, the "Father of our Lord Jesus Christ," who is "able and willing." This is the apostle's confidence "to do unimaginably more than even he and his fellow Christians may ask for or think of."

He, the apostle Paul, sees the whole company of those who bear the name of Christ Jesus as knitted together into one fellowship, whose oneness cannot be dissolved anymore. They belong together. Their oneness is not based on their own initiative and agreement. They are not federates who have arranged and agreed upon a pact of alliance or a treaty that they may cancel as they may wish, and after-

ward nothing will remain. No, they are one family, all be-
gotten by the same Father, the "Father of our Lord Jesus
Christ." They belong together because they all belong to
him as members of his family. This fact, which makes us
and all Christians one family, certainly means that we have
to recognize each other as being brothers and sisters, for
Jesus Christ's sake as people of God, even as the family of
the heavenly Father. This is more than just a parable or an
allegory. The gospel, the "glad tidings of great joy," proclaims that by faith, as believers in Christ Jesus and as
his disciples and followers, we are God's family. We are
God's children—children who were lost but who have
been found and liberated. The Biblical expression "to be
redeemed" means that God sent Christ to pay the ransom
and bring us home. Now we are on our way together, and
on it we find those people who also heard the call of him
who invites everybody to follow.

As we see who these other people are, we may be surprised, and indeed we are. Here we do not choose our
companions, who may even appear to us as a rather queer
lot of people. Christendom is by no means a group of
people who are linked together because of relationship,
descent, friendship, sympathy, learning, culture, or by
common interest and purpose. Here we find a company of
people who at first sight and at first impact impress us as
"strangers and foreigners." This may happen to us nowadays when we attend an ecumenical rally. We are not only
astonished but downright shocked at the great number of
representatives of foreign peoples, of strange and alien
races. Just the same and nevertheless, they claim, and this
claim we have no right to reject, to belong to the family of
our Lord's Father, to the family in which Jesus the Christ
is "the firstborn among many brethren."

You know, and just these last months and weeks have

made it clear once again, how great difficulties can and do arise when this claim, belonging to this family, is brought forward and put into action. This is true for other areas as well; for instance, my country, Germany. For decades, ever since the First World War, when we lost our colonies and with them their native inhabitants, we had thought that we were quite inaccessible to race discrimination because we lived rather secluded from people of foreign origins. But now workers as well as students are pouring in again from foreign countries. In general and in principle they are welcome. Yet the whole picture changes the moment one of them enters a home and asks for a room in which to stay. Then all of a sudden here is the "foreigner," the "stranger," requesting admission to the family circle and thereby producing a problem that needs a decision. Such a decision cannot be made without giving up some accustomed or maybe cherished habits of life. For us, as Christians, and that is to say, as members of our Father's family, the decision that now has to be made and that we would like to make on our own is not left to us. We are meant to act as members of God's family and in conformity with this family's frame of mind, with its spirit. We ought to learn that and actually live up to our Father's wish and will. It is exactly this necessity, this requirement, that causes Paul to pray for the Christian people in Ephesus that the Father may strengthen them "with might by his Spirit in the inner man."

We are always tempted by our old man's nature and indolence to evade our Lord's demands when they become unpleasant and difficult for us. We rather try to find an easier solution or get rid of it altogether. In any case, we look for the least troublesome way out. Yet, we Christians should not do that; certainly not when we are inclined to escape from our duties as members of God's family. For then, very soon we become the ones who find themselves separated, alone and lonely. We cannot but pity Christians, individuals and groups, who try to live their separate lives in order to escape from the growing involvement in the Christian family. It is too large, this Christian family, and therefore they shrink back from the whole family. Their self-concern shows lack of love. Christ is not really the Lord of their lives, and thus they miss their aim and destination. So, what we need again and again is what the apostle asks for as he thinks of his church in Ephesus: that "Christ may dwell in your hearts by faith." For Christ is the one who reveals and imparts his spirit of love to those who receive him, that they, that we, become "rooted and grounded in love." That love which is the atmosphere in the family of God, that love which "believeth all things, hopeth all things, endureth all things," that love comprehends what is the "breadth, and length, and depth, and height." Where we human creatures are being overcome by Christ Jesus dwelling in our hearts—and that means always by his self-sacrificing love—we cannot but welcome to this our family, with joy and gratitude, all fellow creatures who follow his call and join his family.

This joyful experience, when or where it occurs to us on our way, really touches us as a miracle, a miracle of God. But miracles surely are ambiguous in character. They may frighten, or they may delight, those to whom they happen. This miracle here also may do both, but it is up to us which alternative we choose. Believing in Jesus Christ, bound to him in that personal relationship that we call "faith," we see how his followers increase and how faith in him overcomes all barriers between nations and races, even boundaries that have divided Christian confessions for centuries. We cannot but thank God that he in our days is doing "exceeding abundantly above all that we ask or think, according to the power that worketh in us," and to praise and glorify him in Jesus' name!

All of us who are privileged to participate in the World Council of Churches' committees and assemblies should bear witness that this family of God really exists. Personally, I thank God that I did not have to wait for this experience until 1946 when my personal activity and co-operation with this great organization began. There was my fraternal life, together with my three Roman Catholic priest friends, in the Dachau concentration camp in the bunker in the years from 1942 to 1945, and we three altogether were convinced, more than convinced, that we were brothers in God's family. Also, my first ecumenical congregation, in the last few months of the war from December, 1944, to the end of Dachau concentration camp, consisted of persons from different nations, from different confessions and churches, and truly became one family around the one Table of our Lord.

Today all Christian confessions, all continents, and nearly all nations are represented in the World Council of Churches. Our meeting of the Central Committee at Enugu, Nigeria, in January, 1965, clearly convinced me of the genuine family character of our group. The political tensions and controversies keep us still apart, at least in part, and the confessional contrasts have not yet been totally overcome. Nevertheless, our conviction that we all belong to one family of all Christian creeds and traditions no longer meets with scruple, contradiction, and objection. Therefore, we gratefully and gladly join in Paul's praise to God: "Unto him be glory in the church by Christ Jesus throughout all ages, world without end. Amen."

DR. BLAKE CONTINUED

It would be easy in this particular week, as we speak on this inclusive family of God with special regard to race, to center your attention on Selma, Alabama, where all of us have been eyewitnesses these last days of "an American tragedy," as President Johnson referred to it in his press conference last Saturday. But I remind you, as I speak tonight, that this series of dialogue sermons is entitled "An Open Letter to Philadelphia." What I say today will be directed to our Christian obligations here in this city. I do not propose to let you be diverted by your anger at Governor Wallace, if you have some, or his Confederate-bedecked state troopers, or at Sheriff Clark's hoodlums in uniform. I do not propose that you should be diverted by any feelings that you may have against these others from the crisis in race in our own city and in our own churches here.

By way of a necessary aside, let me comment very briefly on the significance of Alabama and the struggle that continues in that state. There are four points, I believe, that are encouraging that rise out of the present crisis in Alabama.

First, I believe it is now clear that the full power of our Federal Government will at last be exerted to enable Negroes in Alabama to register to vote, to vote, and to have their votes counted. This has been long overdue.

Second, I believe that one result of this tragedy will be that no state or city will be able longer to promote the fiction that race relations anywhere are purely a local concern.

Third, I hope that it has now become clear that wherever racial injustice exists (and that is still almost everywhere in our land), the responsibility for violence and disorder rests squarely upon those who block, delay or hinder the establishment of equal racial justice and not upon those who peacefully demonstrate against it.

Fourth, I welcome heartily the entrance into the Selma conflict of a very brave company of white citizens of Alabama led by a Birmingham Lutheran pastor, Missouri Synod, not in the ecumenical movement officially, I remind you. I trust that this company of white Christians will be the advance contingent of a massive mobilization of the members of the still segregated white churches of that state.

These four points are encouraging. The single greatest danger arising out of the Selma tragedy is that we here shall let Selma divert us from Chester, Pennsylvania, or Montgomery from Harrisburg, or the sins of Alabamans from the sins of Philadelphians. It is always easier to stir up hate even among Christians than it is to inspire love and self-sacrifice. So much then for Selma.

Let us return to Philadelphia. What is the situation here? Let me begin with a brief outline of the Christian and Biblical view upon which all church action and all individual Christian action ought to be based. Some of this is repetitive of what has been better said already.

First, our action should be always grounded in the love of Christ. The prayer to which Dr. Niemöller has directed our attention in Eph. 3:14–21 centers upon the Spirit of Christ and the love of Christ. The apostle prays that we be "strengthened with might through his Spirit." He prays that Christ may dwell in our hearts through faith, which is to ask that we as Christians may "be rooted and grounded in love." He prayed further that our comprehension of love may be expanded beyond all the limits that our natural human limitation and our sin impose, that the love of Christ, which is God's kind of love, may fill our lives. This is his prayer. This is the way the apostle indicates, to glorify God through Christ in his church. Let me then remind us all that Christian action under all circumstances must be grounded in Christian love—Christ's kind of love. This is a very practical help in a time of turmoil in race relations, or in any human relations, for that matter. There have been many false prophets who claimed to speak in the name of Jesus Christ, from the first generation until now. And you have available to you a way, I believe, to test the truth of any who names the name of Jesus Christ. Does he exhort to love or to hate? Does he appeal to your fear or to your faith? Does he dwell on others' sins or on our own? If you will use this criteria in your judgments, much of the confusion on race and on other difficult social problems could soon be eliminated from the minds of loyal Christians in our churches everywhere.

Second, there is no limit on Christian love. In the passage that is listed from The Acts of the Apostles (ch. 10:1–46), which was too long to be read in this short service, there is described one of the first successes of the Christian church in this matter of race and ethnic relations. I hope you will want to read it carefully when you go home. I remind you that the people of Israel had long been trained to keep themselves separate and apart from the other races and nations of the world. They had some reasons for trying to be an island of purity in a pagan sea of decadence and idolatry. This they had done despite the universal aspects of their faith in God that inform the whole of the Old Testament prophetic tradition. Jesus was a son of Israel, as was Peter and as was Paul. It was difficult for Peter to break out of the habits and practices of

his own people, his own faith, his own religion, if you
will. These were the habits and practices of the best people in his nation.

And this is our problem here in Philadelphia. The measure of the crisis of the church in Philadelphia is whether,
like Peter, we may be enabled by God to overcome the
walls of ethnic separation that have been built up by
generations of separateness. It requires something of a
miracle to change any white man enough to make him
able even to understand his Negro brothers and sisters in
Christ. And I may remind my Negro brothers and sisters
here that they too require the same miracle of grace in
their hearts if they are to break out of the bitterness and
hatred that is only natural in their situation. But the gospel
of Christ is to loose us all from the natural chains of prej-
udice and fear that so easily and normally and naturally
divide us from one another, and break up his family, which
we profess to be in the church of Jesus Christ. Christian
love has no limits whatever. It is not limited to my family,
my kind, my race, my color, or my nation. Christian love
is indeed very unnatural. It comes by grace alone, through
faith in Jesus Christ. It extends even to our enemies. How
many times shall I forgive? asked Peter of our Lord. Seven
times? That suggestion of seven times revealed even then
at that stage how far Peter had gone, how much he had
been taught by our Lord. For men naturally feel that once
is plenty to forgive and that twice, and then on, is quite
foolish. Peter, beginning to be a Christian, asked, "Seven
times?" And our Lord replied, "No, Peter, seventy times
seven." No limit. No limits to the love of Christ. None at
all.

Third, let us remember that Christian love is action; it
is not mere sentiment, words, feelings, or emotions. A cup

of cold water, a visit to the sick, a visit to a prisoner, a coat for someone who is cold. This is Christian love, and there is no other way to show it. In our efforts to resolve the racial tensions in Philadelphia today (or in any place at any time) we must remember at last that actions in love alone witness to Jesus Christ. And this is important for all of us, no matter what the color of our skin may be, if we wish to witness to Jesus Christ.

If I have persuaded you that this is the Biblical and Christian base upon which our Christian program in Philadelphia must be built, let me be very concrete in the suggestions as to what we in Philadelphia must do to be Christian in our race relations, for we have hardly begun on this matter.

First, I would say, let us worship God together. Pending that day when there will be no segregated congregations, either black or white, let every congregation in this city and in its suburbs resolve to exchange members every Sunday in sufficient quantities that Sunday morning shall no longer be as, dear God, it is true, the most segregated hour of all the week in our land. This requires white congregations to get over their fear and their condescension, and it requires Negro congregations to transcend their hesitations and their bitterness, and this is hard for both. But if we are what we profess to be, this we will do. There are dozen of ways this can be done. It can be planned and executed, if you will. And I have heard until I am sick of it all the reasons given why not to do it. But I am suggesting to you very concretely this afternoon, let us from this Lenten season on worship God together regularly on Sunday morning. I have been delighted all this week that this has been an interracial congregation, but this is not a normal congregation, although I hope you do have always an interracial one here as we do in token in most of our churches now in these great cities. Let us gather around our Communion tables together. Let us regularly approach our altars with our brothers of every color and of every race. This alone makes the Christian congregation at its major gathering for the worship of God able to worship at a time like this.

And second, when we have been at our Lord's Table together, let us desegregate our own tables in our own homes. This some will find much harder, the kind of thing that Dr. Niemöller was saying. Yes, in theory everything is fine until it gets sort of intimate somehow. And then people begin to draw apart in fear—again, on both sides, I would remind you. And so I ask, which will be the first largely white congregation in this city or its environs to announce that they have in fact had Negro guests invited in every household of its membership. This is a thing that can be done if we decide to do it. And which will be the first largely Negro congregation in this city or its environs that will be able to announce that white friends have been welcomed to a meal in each household of its members? I can hear you complain that this is artificial, and that both hosts and guests will be embarrassed. So it is, and so they will be embarrassed.

I am asking you to be embarrassed for Jesus Christ. This is sometimes harder than almost anything else to ask. I am asking rich people, white and black, to smash the social separation based on color that is a part of the tradition of our time and place. And I ask the poorest people in our membership to dare to serve a meal to Christians of another race in their homes, not to make special guests of anybody. Serve as you serve yourselves, even if it means a stand-up meal in a kitchen with too little (and perhaps poorly cooked) food available for guests. I ask everyone to be ready to be brave enough to act like Christians in their homes. I haven't time to develop why this is important, but I can suggest to you that if you do it, you will find something beginning to happen in terms of the fellowship across racial lines in the Christian church of Philadelphia.

Third, let us each one find his place in an organized effort to establish a new public pattern of race relations in this city and its suburbs. Do not think that financial support is enough unless you are very old; then you may get away with that alone. The low level of Christian giving to civil rights organizations, national and local, is a clear mark of the hypocrisy of many of us. But each of us must act beyond giving money. We must join movements and attend dull meetings. We must volunteer our services as tutors and teachers, as demonstrators and letter writers, as speakers and hearers, as voters and civil servants. Such acts alone are adequate expressions of Christian love. To what end? The areas where change is needed are visibly evident. We must desegregate and radically improve the education available for every child in Philadelphia, no matter what the color of his skin. We must eliminate the slums and ghettos and find housing for Negroes and see that they have what they can afford in every section of this city and in every one of its suburbs. We must open up jobs for Negroes in every business enterprise and make it possible for them to be advanced truly and evenly by merit. We must open every institution, public, private, and ecclesiastical to serve men, women, and children without regard to their race or color.

This is no small task. It is not easy. We have hardly begun on it. It is not even at this time evident whether all

Christians who are here in this city acting, as I have suggested, can by their influence alone transform Philadelphia into a place worthy of this name—Philadelphia. But this is our Christian opportunity, as it is our Christian duty. Some of the things I have suggested will require from you and me more courage and more grace than most of us have yet shown. And Christ has not promised that the way of his disciples will be easy, nor even that it will lead to a triumph, except it be by way of a cross.

My dear Christian friends, there is only one way adequately to respond to any sermon on this subject. It is to begin today to act in Christian love. You can find a thousand excuses, as all of us from time to time have done, to go on in the more comfortable pattern of noninvolvement. But I can promise you this: Once involved, you will find, as did Peter and Paul and as have Christians in every place and century, that Jesus Christ himself will meet you on his way and that your life in him will be filled with joy abundant.

THE DIALOGUE

If ever during the course of that great week I felt a moment's disappointment, it was now, as those two magnificent sermons dealing with our foremost problem and concern of the moment rang out through the church. As the microphones were changed from the lectern to the table, I looked about me and was sorry, deeply sorry, to see that not all the pews were crowded with more fellow Americans and fellow Christians. Truly, there was a good showing of light and dark skin side by side, but we wanted more, more to share this great hour with us, more of them to express our oneness in Christ, our equality before him. And more still we wanted a sharing of our determination that this, our foremost American problem, should be solved with nothing but the love of Christ.

We smiled with Dr. Niemöller when he began the dialogue: "Really, Gene, I am at a loss just what question to put to you, for we both know that we are positively of one mind in these matters. When it comes to individual concerns, we can only refer to the great environment, society, and country in which we live with our problems. Our problems in Germany in this respect are comparatively small now.

"On the other hand, the United States of America, in dealing with this very grave problem, is watched by the whole world, as it sets something of an example. People are inclined either to criticize or to follow the lead of the United States. Therefore, I think it is extremely important to see how these things develop and what progress is made. It is a matter of worldwide importance, of common concern. You know that our ecumenical movement has gone through this problem over the last six or seven years. Can you, Gene, tell us something about those churches in South Africa which opposed the Christian World Council in the matter of race? They belonged to the group of Reformed Churches. I think it should be of interest to show the real reasons why the synods of these churches in Transvaal and in the Orange Free State refused to follow their leaders who really were at the brink of consenting to the general attitude of the World Council of Churches, if I remember correctly."

"I think," Dr. Blake said, "that you, Martin, have made the comment on this subject called for by a president of the World Council of Churches. It should be underlined! I said, as far as Birmingham or Alabama was concerned, that nobody can think of this as a local problem, and nobody can think that our national problem is merely 'our problem in the United States.' This thing is worldwide. For in America the indecisiveness on this matter that some of us tend to want to project, the attitude that says, 'Don't go along too fast!' is losing the United States any possibility of being a leader in a free world. This we are losing day by day and month by month. It is no longer a question of 'Sometime we'll have to handle this!'

"As to South Africa, I am a bit uneasy about talking about it, primarily because of a problem that has to do with language. Most of the people in the Dutch Reformed Church in South Africa read Afrikaans and therefore all the news we get about South Africa is in the English press overseas; and the English press has a way of complicating matters because there was that war between Afrikaners and British way back at the beginning of the century, and that is not over yet. This is one of the reasons why the British, the Anglicans if you will, rather enjoy pressing the Afrikaner, who now is the ruler of South Africa, with his failures. And yet it is British money that is almost universal still in terms of the economics. Now here you have this combination of things. Some of the leaders in the Dutch Reformed Church are, as you indicated, as much concerned as any of us could possibly be that their church should make a Christian and Biblical witness, but they are in a similar position to our churches in Alabama and Mississippi, where they feel the dual pressure of culture and government. This is why voting is seen as being so essential in Alabama and Mississippi. These Dutch Reformed elders, who are the ministers of state, sit in pews in Johannesburg and in the capital of the country. This is a terribly difficult thing when they have chosen a way that in my judgment can't be anything but disastrous in the long run.

"Our Government, however, has clearly stated that it has chosen a pattern, a pattern of integration, a pattern of welcoming into the mainstream of American life and freedom all the people who are here. This we have done, and yet, that decision is only a beginning. What I appeal to every Christian congregation in this city and all over our country to do is to make this thing happen in terms of one's inside change, and it will come.

"May I end tonight with just one story. I went to Birmingham, Alabama, last year to the funeral of the little girls who were killed by the bombing there. One of the ministers of my own church had been informed that some of us were coming. This minister told me that he and his wife had for several hours discussed whether he should come out to the airport to meet us. Here was his chance to act according to his convictions. It is almost impossible for some of us to realize that a serious-minded man and his wife would have to discuss it. He made the decision, which was a big decision for him, to come out and meet me and some others. Now this is what happens when you make that kind of decision under God. It just happened, and you can call it chance or it may more properly in this place be called Providence: Who should come down to the airport lobby right after we got off our plane but Martin Luther King and his brother! I introduced our Birmingham people to Martin Luther King. They had not met him; they would not have. But worse, Martin Luther King's brother, who had the car, had to wait for another plane, and Martin Luther King was in a hurry to get to the Gaston Motel in Birmingham. So what happened to this poor minister of my church? He found himself driving Martin Luther King and me to the Gaston Motel. He had taken one little step. He put his body in a place that didn't have any particular danger, and he suddenly found himself maybe losing his job next week; because this could happen!

"It is this kind of thing which is demanded of us all. It may not be a very big step, but it is a first step. But I warn you that if you take the first step, God is not going to let you alone. You will be pushed on until his grace has a chance to transform your Christian life and experience. There is a new joy *anywhere* in that!"

CHAPTER FIVE

POVERTY AND THE NEW JERUSALEM

TEXT: LUKE 6:20–31; MATTHEW 5:3–12
Friday, March 19

DR. NIEMÖLLER BEGAN

This week's last and concluding dialogue service is meant to deal with the issue of poverty. Surely this human need and misery has been, and still is, the permanent companion of mankind on its way through history, unchangeable and insuperable as it seems to be, for the Lord himself says, "Ye have the poor always with you." Needless to say, this statement does not and cannot remove, nor even reduce, our obligation to fight this human suffering, for it constantly appeals to our innate empathy. At present, it is especially obvious and urgent. We know much more than any previous generation how general and universal the burden and the pressure of poverty have become. As I mentioned Wednesday evening when I spoke of economics, far more than half of the present world population are too poor to satisfy their hunger. This is a very, very grave and serious matter, not only for those who are

hungry, but for all Christendom, for all who know Jesus
as being the Christ, the one who will come "to judge the
quick and the dead." He is the one who suffers. He suffers
where people are stricken with poverty, and we are the
ones who make him suffer, for he will say, "I was ahun-
gered, and ye gave me no meat." The realm of poverty,
this area which is a very, very grave and serious matter of
which we have knowledge, has widened the world over.
The poor, once far away, of whom our fathers didn't know
anything, have become near to us. They have become our
neighbors. They have entered into the sphere of our responsibility. Our chances to help, our opportunities, as
they were expressed in the general theme of this week,
have multiplied. They have increased, which is to say that
we cannot, we must not, shut our eyes or close our minds
to their poverty and their wants. We Christians know this,
and being Christians, we may not pass by this responsibility. To deny this responsibility means the denial of Him
whom we claim to be our Savior and Lord. The campaign
against poverty will have to continue and will remain a
permanent companion of Christendom in this world, if we
walk through life in the footsteps of the Master.

In 1952, when I visited the Russian Orthodox Church in
Moscow for the first time, I was really surprised to find
crippled beggars asking for alms in the narthex of every
church that was in use. There were no beggars anywhere
in the streets of Moscow, for no begging was allowed. But
the churches could not do without them, for they needed
them as symbols, reminding the Christian people of their
liability to them who are in need of service and help. In
all "Christian" and formerly "Christian" countries, state
and community have taken over the care of the poor, the
fight against poverty. We, as the church, after having done

our service and after having shown, caused, and initiated this common human duty and obligation to man and society, now have to do the same service to those neighbors who were far away, but have become near. Once more and still: "Ye have the poor always with you." For this, then, we, Christians and churches, must be on our guard, for Jesus' sake: that the poor are being cared for; it is and it will always be our business and our concern, because this is our opportunity. Actually it is the only one we have to serve our Lord and to thank him for his love and his sacrifice for our sake. We can show our solidarity with and extend our aid and assistance to them with whom he identifies himself. Certainly this door is wide open and will stay so until the "holy city," the "new Jerusalem" that John envisions, will come down, and "there shall be no more death, neither sorrow, nor crying, neither shall there be any more pain."

We have listened again to the Beatitudes of our Lord as they are handed down to us in the Gospels bearing the names of Matthew and Luke, respectively. In both versions the "poor" are the first ones to be called "blessed," and in both wordings they are told that theirs is the "kingdom." There will be a fulfillment when the Lord comes in his power and glory and when "the former things are passed away." The author of The Gospel According to Luke, in quoting Jesus, is thinking of the state of poverty that his eyes see, of those poor who suffer from hunger and want, who need their bread and need it now! Woe to them who are rich and full now, who do not recognize their opportunity that they may help the needy, and that in doing so pass through the open door and take the way that will lead to genuine and real fulfillment. If they don't recognize it and they pass by the fellowman's need, they will miss their goal and find their life emptied and lost, their fate worse, much worse even than that of the poor who may wait in hope and trust in the Lord's promise.

We Christians are called upon here in the context of Luke's Gospel that we make the right, the Christian use of that which God has entrusted to us. This refers—we may have heard it with some surprise—not to our material goods alone, which we ought to share with those who are materially poor, but we are also summoned to let others share in the benefit of the gifts of the Spirit. We receive love for hatred, forgiveness for sin, mercy for legal claim. To act as he acts toward us, that is what Jesus expects us to do to others. So, Luke's Beatitudes are not really opposed to or different from Matthew's text (as you might think if you compare them), which says, "Blessed are the poor in spirit"! Poor in spirit means that we, trusting in our own righteousness, in our system of morals and ethics, are by no means as rich and full as we may think. On the contrary, we have to acknowledge our spiritual deficiency. We have to admit our poverty in real spirit and our need of the Spirit of Christ in order to be counted among those whom Jesus calls "blessed." To love our enemies, to bless them that curse us, to offer the other cheek to him who smites us, that is what Jesus means when he speaks of the poor in spirit and declares them to be "blessed." To those who in this sense are "poor in spirit," he opens the prospect, even the title and claim, to God's "kingdom of heaven."

My Christian friends, this week the Open Letter to the Christian Church in Philadelphia has been on our mind. We have tried to draw connecting lines from the once young, but now rather old and nearly extinct church of the first century in Asia Minor to our Christian church which we represent here and now and which lives still awaiting the end of this confused and nearly impenetrable phase of mankind's history.

Yet, there is a word of God that wants to be heard by every human creature. Our Lord himself designates it "the word of my patience." This word carries his promise for those who have kept, who keep, and will keep it: "Him that overcometh will I make a pillar in the temple of my God." Who is he that overcomes? To overcome—this has nothing to do with what we mortals might call a "victory" in our sense of the word—is not accomplished by might nor by power. It is meant for and granted to those whom Jesus calls "blessed" and of whom we read in James's epistle, "Behold, we count them happy which endure." They are the "poor in spirit" who trust in Jesus, not in themselves, and who follow him. They become the citizens of the New Jerusalem, the city in which Christ Jesus reigns as King and Lord of all. And these are the glad tidings of great joy that must and shall go with us, that put us to work in his Kingdom, in his service for his brothers and our own, for we belong to him. My friends, "blessed are they who belong to him"! Amen.

DR. BLAKE CONCLUDED

We have been speaking this week, trying to persuade you who are leaders and pillars of the church in Philadelphia to follow that vision which has come to the church of Jesus Christ worldwide through the open door of the ecumenical movement of our time. The burden of much of what we have said has been to ask you to move out from the safe and comfortable tradition of the churches into the center of the stream of human history, to serve Jesus Christ your Lord in the world for which he died, to risk your lives and the life of the church itself in the many-fronted battle in which the loyal army of Jesus is now engaged.

This challenge has seemed strange to some of you, I know. You have wondered whether this ecumenical movement is not a diversion from the Biblical truth that you have been taught from your youth and even possibly a heresy, such as the New Testament predicts will come in the last times.

I was brought up in a Presbyterian home in which "dispensational theology" was the understanding of the gospel. And although I do not exactly interpret or understand the Scriptures as my parents did, I want you to know that I still believe, as I was taught in my youth, that the Second Coming of Jesus Christ is an important and vital part of the full rounding of Christian faith. In order to make this as clear to you as I can, I want to speak, on the one hand, about the challenge to the church of Jesus Christ that is posed by President Johnson's dream and program of "the Great Society," and on the other hand, to talk to you about the New Jerusalem that comes down from God out of heaven, the vision of the "last things," which was the preoccupation of the presbyter John, who wrote the book of Revelation, upon part of which these sermons have been based.

One of the most exciting things that has happened in our time recently is the vision that our President has articulated in talking about the Great Society. I realize full well that most of my fellow Republicans in this city of Philadelphia are highly suspicious of what appears to be but the latest of a series of slogans of the Democratic Party, in the succession of the New Deal, the Square Deal, and the New Frontier. But there is something in this expression "the Great Society" that can transcend partisan politics if the Christians in the United States of America are able to catch a vision of what is really possible, as it never was before, namely, to do away with the heavy burden of poverty in our land.

What I hope and pray will happen is that in these next months and years, the Christians of the United States will decide that to allow poverty to continue, either in great cities like Philadelphia or in the rural areas such as the Appalachian region or the Southwest—to allow this to continue is simply immoral in view of our wealth, in view of our capital, and in view of our tremendous productive capacity of the things that human beings need. It used to be that poverty was inevitable, and in a sense, it is always inevitable, as Dr. Niemöller has said. But in the old days it was inevitable because of the technological deficiencies of men. Now that part of it can be eliminated. People don't have to be poor any longer if we decide that we really want to direct the products of our machines to meet the legitimate needs and desires of people, all our people. The excitement of the concept of the Great Society is in its vision of what can happen now on this earth if we decide to use our technological skills to make it happen here among us.

But I am sure that many members of our churches, ministers and lay people, are troubled by the idea of the church in any way identifying its program with so "worldly" an end. Is this not a new form of materialism being insinuated into what ought to be somehow a much more spiritual purpose of the church of Jesus Christ? Our Lord said, "The poor you have always with you." How can a Christian then assert that we ought to eliminate this burden of poverty from our land and, with foreign aid, from the whole world as soon as possible? Did not Jesus say, "Blessed are you poor, for yours is the kingdom of God"? How can the involvement of the church in a material effort, if there are such spiritual values of poverty, be justified?

And there is even a further complication. Is not the church of Jesus Christ really and basically ultimately concerned with eternal life in heaven? Is it not wrong for us to get so much involved in the worldly ends that are the business of governments and states that we forget what the church and the gospel are really about?

These are not small questions. They cannot be brushed away. And yet I remind you that Jesus himself, by word and example, taught those who followed him to express a highly spiritual faith in very concrete and material ways. You can love God only if you love your neighbor, which means to minister to all his needs, including food and shelter and clothing. In the parable of the good Samaritan, one clear part of its teaching is the criticism especially of religious people who pass by so easily on the other side when they see a brother man in physical need. It is well known that there is no subject about which Jesus spoke so often as he did about money and its use here and now.

We seem to be in a dilemma. We are clearly wrong if we understand Christianity as simply a stimulus to earthly economic accomplishment, as if man's salvation could be measured by the number of calories in his diet, the number of televisions he has to amuse himself with. But we are just as clearly wrong if we become so otherworldly that we prove the communists right when they charge us with preaching a gospel designed to be an opiate of the people, quieting the revolutionary urges of the poor with promises of "pie in the sky, by and by."

I wonder if I have said enough to persuade you to look at the fundamental paradox of the gospel. A paradox is, as you know, a seeming contradiction. The truth about Christian purpose and program can only be understood in accepting at the same time what appears to be a flat contradiction—a paradox.

Jesus himself often taught in paradox. He said, "The kingdom of heaven is at hand." The Kingdom is among you and within you. But he also taught us to pray, as we have just now, "Thy kingdom come." Jesus was at once the most materialistic religious teacher who ever lived and at the same time he said, "My kingdom is not of this world." This paradox is our Lord's own paradox. We distort what he was and what he taught unless we accept somehow all of what he taught us and all of the God whom he revealed even upon a cross, which (another paradox) is at the same time both a symbol of failure and death and a sign of victory and hope.

Our trouble is that almost all of us are so much creatures of our own cultural and popular thought forms that we try to do something quite impossible, namely, to compress Jesus Christ into a sort of evolutionary new Jerusalem that man by his own efforts and his own technology will at last create upon this earth. But it is perfectly clear, if you will read the New Testament, that the first Christians had no such idea at all.

They looked for Jesus to come again. They looked for God, by his consummating act, to bring all of this human history to a glorious end by establishing by his power a new heaven and a new earth.

The burden of this closing sermon is to say to you that unless we learn somehow to accept both sides of this paradox, we will distort the good news of the gospel of Jesus Christ. For this is the good news: That God has intervened in human history by sending his Son into the world, incarnate in human flesh. He was born of the Virgin Mary, suffered under Pontius Pilate, died and was buried. And he rose again—and he shall come again. This too is a part of the Christian creed and the gospel of man's salvation.

But this does not mean that Christians then turn their backs upon the problems of daily life. Rather, the opposite happens. Because of Jesus Christ and his victory over sin and death, it is his disciples who dare in faith to take upon themselves the burden of the hungry and suffering world and find in such undertaking the abundant life now which he promised to the faithful.

To be a good citizen upon this earth, you must be essentially a citizen of heaven. To give yourself to establish God's Kingdom on earth, you need to have faith that it is God who is establishing it, however dark appears the way before you. It is not a chance coincidence that Francis of Assisi, who embraced poverty as his chosen way of life, taught us Christians better than any other since our Lord himself walked among us the joy of life upon God's good earth and the beatitude of giving rather than receiving. It is not by chance that the authentic, recognizable saints among us are always those who give themselves to the poor, the alien, the outcast, generously sharing all material goods with all who need them; and yet their faces are lifted up toward heaven in expectation of the coming of the Lord.

This paradox is the secret of Christian courage in times of trouble and of Christian humility in times of accomplishment and success. John wrote, "In the Spirit he carried me away to a great, high mountain, and showed me the holy city Jerusalem coming down out of heaven from God." And to the church in Philadelphia the same John wrote: "I am coming soon; hold fast what you have, so that no one may seize your crown. He who conquers, . . . I will write on him the name of my God, and the name of the city of my God, the new Jerusalem which comes down from my God out of heaven. . . . He who has an ear, let him hear what the Spirit says to the churches."

THE DIALOGUE

The final dialogue brought anything but a peaceful conclusion to the wealth of thought that had been showered upon us during the week. There was, finally, a discrepancy of thought. When Dr. Blake joined Dr. Niemöller at the table, for the last time we sadly felt, he was cheerfully taken to task. "Gene," Dr. Niemöller mused, "there is that question of the paradox. I am not so sure whether we should bring it up on this last evening, but I would like to see it clarified a bit because really I have never quite understood it. I struggled through this even with my friend, Karl Barth. I just don't see it, don't find a paradox. I think a practical Christian life is a part of social existence that makes itself felt!"

"I am glad you put me in Karl Barth's class when you disagree with me," Dr. Blake laughed. "At least that gives me a little encouragement. The point that I am trying to make," and he smiled, "I am not so sure you don't understand it, is that if you talk about Christianity in terms of 'here and now' entirely, the Christian, like other men, is dependent upon his own strength and his own very human hopes. And if you talk about Christianity in terms of future only, and the heavenly reward, this kind of faith becomes so easily the excuse for the Christian to turn his back upon his brother and this world. Now, I think I understand—see if I do—what you said the other day, for I was listening carefully. You, I think, would say that it is neither a future nor an earthly contrast; rather, that it is the eternal relationship with Jesus Christ right now that is Christianity—and there is no contradiction in this."

Dr. Niemöller nodded approval, and Dr. Blake continued: "If that is so, I think all you are saying is that (better than most of us) you have been able to identify your spiritual insight with your daily duty. This is the doctrine (the technical term for it is 'realized eschatology')—that is to say, the doctrine of the last things—which I was talking about, transforming the present moment into one that is in the true sense both spiritual and material. Is that a fair statement of what you would say in correction of me?"

"I think it is," Dr. Niemöller replied. "However, there is one link still missing in the construction of this chain; namely—and I am deeply convinced of this, owing to what we have lived through in our generation—that the teachings of Jesus, the ethical message of the Sermon on the Mount, is not in any contrast to the realities of this world. I have learned to believe that really loving your enemy is better politics than hating him. Hating the enemy creates enmity, whereas there is one chance, God's chance, in loving the enemy, the chance of overcoming both the enemy and the enmity. Insofar I really do not agree with this paradoxical concept of what Christianity basically is, or is supposed to be, or is represented as being. I always think of the good old Christian woman who never studied theology and never thinks on these two things becoming a paradox. The normal person interprets or understands this only as 'truth speaking against truth.' They are not speaking against each other. They are really blending into one. The ultimate question is just whether we recognize the oneness of these seemingly antagonistic and contradictory truths!"

Dr. Blake, grinning widely, commented: "You did a mean trick to me then, though! You inserted into my position the idea that I would say that on this earth it wasn't practical to love your enemy. This was the paradox! Now this one was getting at me in an unfair fashion! I am not sure," he continued more pensively, "that I agree that always the Christian way is the practical way. But I will say this: I think it is always the right way, the right way that yet leads to a cross, as you well know. It does not always work. We Americans like things that work, and it doesn't always follow that people are won by this Christian spirit. I will agree with you thoroughly that there is no other way to peace; there is no other way to joy; there is no other way to righteousness except in this way. And my contrast is not what is practical and what is impractical. The paradox—this woman that you talk about—this simple woman lives with paradoxes. She believes in school for the children; she sends them there hoping that the environment will teach them something more than she is able to do. She also punishes the child from time to time to direct him in the way. Society has both schools and prisons. One of them says human beings are responsible, and the other one says human beings can be controlled by an environment. You push them, and you hold them responsible, and this is a paradox. I am responsible, and yet I am the product of what my environment has made me."

"Certainly," Dr. Niemöller agreed, "because God created man as an individual and as a social being, we have this original paradox, but I should say this paradox is in ourselves and not in what we have to live and what life means to us."

Dr. Blake concluded: "I would agree that if because of the paradox one then doesn't know how to live—that is to say, one side of the truth would drive him to retreat from the world and the other side would drive him into the world, I think that is a misunderstanding of the truth. I only hope that ultimately I, and all of us here, can transcend that paradox as you in your life have done!"

At that, we all arose. Our thoughts, emotions, our gratitude for the wealth of experience of this week all became manifest as we sang together "Our God, Our Help in Ages Past, Our Hope for Years to Come."

It was the family of God in Christ Jesus singing, affirming the faith.

The minister gave the final benediction from the altar:

"Eternal and everloving Father, for the blessings of this week together, we give thee thanks. For the messages and spirits of these two servants of thine we are grateful. As these services of worship come to an end may our service to thee begin. And now may we all: 'Go forth into the world in peace, be of good courage; hold fast that which is good, render to no man evil for evil; strengthen the fainthearted; support the weak, help the afflicted; honor all men; love and serve the Lord, rejoicing in the power of the Holy Spirit.'" Then, the Reverend Mrs. Elizabeth W. Fenske, of the United Church of Christ, closed her prayer with the blessing:

"The grace of the Lord Jesus Christ, and the love of God, and the fellowship of the Holy Spirit be with you all. Amen."

CHAPTER SIX

THE PUBLIC DISCUSSION AT THE FIRST PRESBYTERIAN CHURCH

———————

The dinner at the First Presbyterian Church on Friday night was the concluding event. It had been arranged to provide the setting for a public discussion of the week that had transpired. No question period had been held on any of the five days, for these gatherings were meant to be, above all else, services of worship.

One hundred and fifty people had made reservations and broke the bread together. The women of the church served a fine meal with pleasant efficiency, and Dr. J. Ernest Somerville, the minister, was our host and master of ceremonies. In a "perrfecktly" Scottish accent he bade us a warm welcome.

To this gathering of people representing more different denominations than we shall ever know, festive in mood, relaxed in manner, and given to the unifying joy of laughter, Dr. Somerville read the first question: "The first one we have," he said, "is a fairly general one addressed to you, Dr. Niemöller. 'In your travels over America this year, have you seen evidence of a decline or a growing in spiritual vitality in the United States churches?'"

"I don't think I can answer that question," Dr. Niemöller said, "because on this trip, so far, I have been here three weeks only. Most of this time was spent in seminaries . . ." The rest was drowned in laughter that continued when Dr. Somerville, with a broad grin, ad-libbed: "Dr. Blake, in your travels over America . . ."

But then Dr. Blake replied: "The church is not as turned in upon itself as it was two years ago in America. This is a change; it is, I think, probably more upset, but that proves it is *alive!*"

Dr. Somerville turned to Dr. Niemöller. " 'I may have misunderstood,' says this questioner, 'but on Tuesday I heard you say that we need to experiment more with the Christian faith. If this is what you said, would you please elaborate?' "

Dr. Niemöller answered: "This is what I wanted to express Tuesday night. We have to practice our faith more, not just think and talk about it. We have to live it. To live our faith as a Christian is often regarded as a daring enterprise. I had wanted to underline that faith is not something that can be finished up by thinking. It has to be related and applied to life as we face life and live it."

There was agreement all around. The next question was particularly addressed to Dr. Blake. Its reading was accompanied by good-natured laughter: " 'Do you feel that Christian principles will have to be modified to suit the affluent Great Society?' "

Dr. Blake retorted: "What really bothers me when I read the New Testament are such verses as, 'It is easier for a camel to go through the eye of a needle than for a rich man to enter the kingdom of God.' I say this bothers me because most of us in this room, not all perhaps, but most of us, are richer in things than almost anybody living in Palestine at the time Jesus said these words. This is the problem that I was quite inadequately struggling with this afternoon. 'The poor you have always with you.' 'Blessed are you poor, for yours is the kingdom of heaven.' And yet, you cannot take that and say, 'Well, then let's keep as many people poor as possible, and this is the way blessedness comes!' That is obviously a distortion of what Jesus meant. Therefore, despite Dr. Niemöller this afternoon, I think you have got to have two contradictory things, and you say them all the time.

"Of course, it is true that no one can be expected to respond to the gospel who is at that moment starving to death. I am thinking of D. T. Niles, who is one of the great Christian leaders today. Some of us, sitting together in discussions about missionary policy, used the expression of a 'rice Christian,' a rice Christian being one who came and listened to the sermons in order to get food to eat. D. T. Niles said: 'Be a little careful of that! My grandfather was a rice Christian. He was starving to death. That is the reason he came, and that is the reason I am a Christian.'

"Now, it is both the material and the meaning of the material in which Christianity is involved. It is not simply a spiritual religion. The real question is how with so much goods and such affluence things do not become your God. It is the idolatry of the Old Testament in new forms!"

The subject of poverty was not exhausted yet. Dr. Somerville combined the next two questions, related as they were, and addressed them to Dr. Niemöller: "'Why is it that poverty does follow the Christian world when we are able in non-Christian terms to deal with it? Is it a part of the Christian church and inescapable therefore?'" And the other one:"'Since charity openly condemns poverty, isn't the saying, "The poor you have with you always" then an admission of defeatism?' "

Dr. Niemöller looked up as if puzzled. Dr. Somerville took it as if Dr. Niemöller had not understood and he volunteered: "When you tell a German something in a Scot's accent, you see it gets . . ." Again, there was a wave of warm laughter to which Dr. Niemöller began to reply.

"We have a saying in German," he said, " 'Why say a thing simply when you can say it complicatedly?' " But then he continued: " 'The poor you always have with you.' Jesus says it to his disciples when some of them think it more urgent to care for the moment about the poor people than to care for Jesus at the time he is about to die. He says, 'You will have time for the poor, but my time with you is limited.'

"I did not quite get the question," Dr. Niemöller inserted. "I see no defeatism here. The poor are always with you. This is a task which follows you and will accompany you all through your life and your children's lives as well, and so on. And to act for the poor, where can there be any doubt when we see a person suffering from his poverty? As a Christian, I am responding to the appeal of Christ, who is appealing to me as the one who identifies himself with the person suffering from poverty. Where is there defeatism?"

He repeated the first question, " 'Why is it that poverty does follow the Christian world when we are able in non-Christian terms to deal with it? Is it a part of the Christian church and unescapable therefore?' Of course we can deal with poverty," he summarized, "certainly we can! The question is, who *does*? Are we thinking about it and knowing that the medicine is there? And let it go at that? A story comes to mind about myself. You see, I have not been sick a day in my life, but sometimes the doctor came and prescribed something that I ought to take. So, somebody goes to the drugstore and buys the medicine. You can find it in my room today, all of it. I never took it.

"To deal with poverty, having the right prescription, that is not the question. But whether you really do it! take it! exercise it!" Amid the laughter and warm applause to his story he added this statement: "No matter who else cares for the poor, our Christian obligation will always remain, will never cease."

The next two questions moved into another area, "perhaps not unrelated though," as Dr. Somerville put it. He turned to Dr. Blake: " 'How can Christians deal effectively with their Jewish friends concerning presentation of the Christian message with the view to conversion? Should the effort be made in the first place?' " Dr. Somerville also read the second question, which seemed to have at least some relation to the first: " 'In regard to syncretism, how does one relate to non-Christians?' "

Dr. Blake answered. "I would rather have replied to this first question about six months hence. I have accepted the invitation from some Jewish friends in St. Paul to give a lecture there on this subject and I think it needs to be talked about. That is the reason I said I would go. Here is one very interesting thing: The Second Vatican Council was struggling, as you know, to say what it wanted to say about the relationship of the Jewish people and the Roman Catholic Church. We read in the press that there was a tendency at one time to put this into the chapter on ecumenical relations. The council said: 'That does not belong there. Jews are not Christians, and the term "ecumenical" means the whole of the inhabited world under Christ.' So then they said: 'Well, let's discuss it in connection with Islam and Buddhism and other "high religions." Isn't that the place to put it?'—and equally this is wrong.

"I was discussing this subject with Dr. Visser 't Hooft down in Buenos Aires about five or six years ago. Dr. Niemöller was there, and a friend of mine and I were talking about it. This was the gist of it. In American culture it is true that you are not supposed to proselytize, that is to say, if someone is a Catholic, you don't as a Protestant go to him and say, 'I think your religion is wrong'; in a drawing room you accept each other. This is our courteous treatment of groups, and in part it is what a pluralistic society requires to have peace. But the fact is that neither Judaism nor Christianity is fully lived unless it is trying to win people to the other's faith. They are so similar that it is more difficult to preach the gospel to a Jew than it is to preach it to someone who has never heard of it. The difficulty is the intimacy.

"What I am going to be doing myself before I give this lecture is to make a restudy particularly of the latter part of the Epistle to the Romans, for it was Dr. Visser 't Hooft down in Buenos Aires who said in irritation to me and another American colleague: 'The trouble with you Americans is you don't believe Romans!' What he was basically saying is that one of the descriptions of the Christian church is the New Israel. That is to say, it is a continuance of God's people that begins in the Old Testament. Now, all of us know that Marcion was a heretic. He wanted to get rid of the Old Testament. Yet still in certain Arab Christian countries now they want to get rid of it again. You cannot understand the New Testament without the Old Testament. This is clear. But can you treat members of the old Israel as you do other non-Christians? I am not talking about race or ethnic matters. I am talking now about people who are a part of the faithful of Israel. These people I think—and here is the end of it—need to be won as a community rather than picked off one by one. I think in that process we who are Christian will learn a great deal about God too."

"Would you care to comment, Dr. Niemöller?" Dr. Somerville asked.

"Yes, I should like to," Dr. Niemöller replied. "Naturally, I have concerned myself with this in Germany a great deal and had to speak on it also. What I want to say—maybe I can help my good friend, Gene, with it too—is this: I always tell the Jews who want me to speak to them that the ethics of Judaism and of Christianity are one hundred percent the same—the ethics. The only question is how to live these ethics. Who helps you to live these ethics? That is the Savior, that is the Messiah. The law is the same. What Jesus explains in the Sermon on the Mount is but a definition of Judaic law, strictly speaking. This is shared by numerous Jewish scribes in the following centuries who are teaching just the same. There is no contrast in the ethics, only in the fulfillment of God's law. Who fulfills the law of God? Not man—he is a sinner. Who redeems from sin? Who, and who alone, makes people really to fulfill what God wants them to do?"

Dr. Niemöller's forceful questions created a moment of special pensiveness among the audience. Dr. Somerville read the next question, which seemed to tie up with the thoughts of the moment: " 'Dr. Niemöller, is there any danger that the Nazi leaders during Hitler's time who are now in leading positions in West Germany will again form a threat to the free world?' "

Dr. Niemöller: "There are no Nazis even near a leading position in Germany. This is what I am angry about: We have hundreds of judges in legal and court institutions in Western Germany whose background nobody knows. They have never told, or confessed, that they were Nazis, and that they have officiated in this or that trial in a manner to which today nobody would agree. The same applies to the police. Police and judges are mutually keeping each other in their positions and nobody is trying to change that. Therefore, I am very much for the prolongation of a possibility to prosecute these people. I do not so much want to see them removed from leading positions in terms of punishment. I want the law system in Western Germany freed from this poisoning!"

The next question was addressed to Dr. Blake and took us back to the domestic scene: "Why was the church silent in championing human dignity in reference to race until after the Supreme Court spoke?"

"The church was not silent," Dr. Blake replied. "In fact, we were criticized for twenty or thirty years for making entirely too many pronouncements on the subject. The core of the problem was that we said all the right things. I forget what year the nonsegregated church in the nonsegregated society was accepted as what we believed in. No one paid any attention to it because there was no fighting in the streets at that time. This was just a statement by the General Assembly or the General Convention or whichever church to which you belonged. It was saying all the right things. What happened—and frankly, in part it happened because of television—was one of the things that television does: it induces spontaneous reaction all over this country. The Commission on Religion and Race of the National Council of Churches spent most of its time last week discouraging people from going to Alabama— not whipping them up to go. We don't want any more of them down there now (Governor Wallace does not want them there for different reasons!), because we don't want things to get out of hand and people to get hurt to no good end. The fact is that the churches are slow in seeing this, compared to the Negro civil rights leaders.

"But I'd like to say something about where I think some of the heart of it was—the start of this. If you go across the Southland, a great deal of the leadership for civil rights is in the Negro community in the South. And if you want to know where those people met and where they got their songs that they sing and where they got what it takes to be beaten, it is in churches all over the South. Now you see that the way the question is asked here indicates how white we think. It is the white churches that were very slow. Not the church of Jesus Christ. The young people—where do they learn it, where do they meet?—you'll find them meeting in the churches all across the land. This, I think, is no help to me, a white minister in a largely white church; but the fact is that in the spring of 1963 you had to begin to act.

"The actions have been all kinds of actions. Some of them very little ones. But somebody came off the fence to say, 'I stand here'—this is the reason that I suggested yesterday in the sermon this very simple thing of inviting people of another race to your home. One of our questions shows that somebody is angry about this, I think. Why? Not that this solves anything. It could be a horrible occasion for the inviter and the invitee. Negroes are not waiting for your and my invitations to come to our houses. This is not the point. The point is that somehow we must actually move some bodies into that kind of thing from here to there. Actually this is the way that the new pattern of race relations will be begun. It is not a simple problem to change social patterns and social thinking, but I suggest to you that the church is one of the places where the ideas and the examples are being put forward. During the March on Washington I said we were 'late, very late in coming'— with our bodies that is, not late with the theory. We have had the theory always, but we were late in coming. That makes a vast difference in terms.

"The movement itself now has been desegregated. That is an advance. It was, for a time, almost entirely composed of people being discriminated against, demanding their rights from a government and from a people who were discriminating against them. Since the March on Washington, August 28, 1963, this movement has been a movement of Americans demanding the rights of all Americans. This is what I hope the church will understand increasingly as time goes on."

A wave of applause expressed both approval and appreciation to Dr. Blake. But with time not standing still, Dr. Somerville posed this related question to Dr. Niemöller: " 'With the United States racial strife in mind, should the Christian answer of personal commitment and love necessarily always be permissive? Doesn't this permissiveness at times work to the disadvantage of all involved, when we remember the reality of the nature of man?' "

We were not quite sure what the questioner really meant. But Dr. Niemöller gave this reply: "I think it is really a mandate and a task for the Christian church to see to it that things are being done on the spur of the moment, on her own initiative, until a public opinion has been created. For instance, as to looking after the poor, that the state or the community has become responsible and acknowledges this responsibility that so far was done by the voluntary care of Christian people, Christian congregations and churches. I think this kind of voluntary initiative on the part of the church is a step toward legal fixation of matters of care, and I think that such voluntary action is also needed in the matter of racial strife."

Dr. Somerville asked Dr. Blake if he would care to comment on this any further.

Dr. Blake smiled as he said: "I understood the answer, and the answer is all right, but I am not certain I understood the question. Dr. Niemöller correctly stated that voluntarism is mandatory. We have been criticized from time to time for spending too much of our church effort on changing laws. As people have said, 'Don't you know that you cannot force people to be good and that the proper thing is to preach and have them respond in love?' Everyone knows that, so it didn't need to be urged, even upon those of us who were concerned that the church's influence, if it had any, on the law-making process in our nation might be used to give people the justice that the constitutional documents guarantee. However, it does seem to me—and I have been saying it for the last eight months, after the comprehensive law was passed last June —that the church's task with regard to race falls much more heavily on the voluntary things that we are normally geared to do. It is really a conversion problem. It is just as difficult to get people to respond differently when they have been brought up in isolation and in fear, as it is to turn from absolute selfishness to Christlike self-sacrifice.

"I think it is true in what we have normally thought about as 'repentance unto life' or conversion, that often the outward step is a very small one. It can be just the turning of direction, which the Greek word indicates. You are still where you were before, but which way you are going is very important, always as important as where you are. For in the long run, the faith is crucial. Therefore, I am very anxious that our churches should try as concretely as they can to build the right relationships within the context of the church.

"Let me tell one story of very long ago when I was chairman of an interracial commission in Southern California. The city fathers had lost a lawsuit to the NAACP. It was about 1939 when the lawsuit won by the NAACP forced the city fathers to modify their normal program of the segregation of the municipal swimming pool. They responded by closing the pool. This, when it was 110 degrees in the summertime in Pasadena, was the best creative solution that the city fathers found after they lost the lawsuit to the NAACP.

"Now, if you just conjure up a little imagination, think of what that meant to the Negro community, just in frustration if nothing else. Oh, gradually the pool was opened on a nonsegregated basis, and none of the horrible things happened that were predicted. It was that long ago, in that part of the country, where the first Negro schoolteacher was hired. The first Negro policeman was hired. The first Negroes were put behind counters in stores. All of this which now we have seen in national tension, this part of the country had to do then.

"I give this background to say that one of the most educated and most attractive members of the commission that had been set up, which I had the honor to chair, was a Negro woman better educated than most of us. She was a graduate of the University of Edinburgh. But she had a job in the school system in the health department. I am not going to detail what she was there for. She would have been teaching in the high school probably, if it had not been for her color.

"We were having our annual meeting one night, sitting around the table. Someone brought a cake, and we were eating it and drinking coffee and commenting upon our experience. We had been together about three years then, had had some battles, and we had gotten whipped from both sides on everything. In fact, we were accused of stirring up the problem. There wouldn't have been any problem if we hadn't stirred it up, was the theory. (This is Governor Wallace's feeling, too, I am sure.)

"The Negro woman then said something I have never forgotten. She said: 'You know, I have enjoyed meeting once a month with this group. I don't have normal opportunity to meet any nice white people.' If you will think what that means, you will begin to act on the subject."

There was a great quiet among us as we listened to the wealth of thought and surveyed our own attitudes in terms of what we had heard. It was a very human, a natural reaction which found us, moments later, laughing out loud and happy when Dr. Somerville, friend from Scotland, introduced the next question with his own personal commentary.

"This is, I think, in some sense a related question and as a loyal subject of Queen Elizabeth who remembers George Washington and all his cohorts, I take some delight in this question: 'Both speakers evidently feel it is Christian at times to break the civil law. Who determines at what point it is right to put your opinion above the lawmakers by direct action rather than by an attempt to change the law through the democratic process?' "

"You start, Martin; I'll follow," Dr. Blake said swiftly and caused another wave of warm laughter that was augmented by applause when Dr. Niemöller began: "I see no problem!" He went on to say: "I have said this before in one of the sermons of the last three days: the moment I become sure of something that the state wants me to do, be it by law or by order, but it is of such nature that I am sure Jesus Christ would say *no* to it, I know also that he will leave me, let me alone, should I oblige and obey. So then I do not obey and need not obey, because one must obey God rather than man. This is a simple thing! A much more difficult and complicated problem arises when it comes to what positive stand to take in politics and in matters concerning the life of a nation. The basic question remains the same. To illustrate the point let me tell the story that I have often told before. It was near the end of the First World War. I was in command of a submarine, and my duty was to attack an enemy convoy. We were submerged, and I was alone in the turret with the navigator, who had to help me in various ways and finally to relay my order to the torpedo room, to push that button when I would say, 'Let go!' What if that navigator would have been Jesus, standing next to me, receiving and carrying out my orders to push that button? Can I imagine that? I did not know it then but have come to know it: if Jesus cannot participate in what I am doing, I am out of faith. Faith means to follow Christ. Faith is not an opinion or conviction; faith is life. This is my answer to that question."

Dr. Blake had this to say: "All of us have been taught that order is important in this society. In a city like this, to have law and order is terribly important. Any of us who have been in a place where there is a revolution going on will know that there are tremendous values just in having police that keep things quiet. It has nothing to do with justice or injustice—just order. Now, therefore, this question of order is raised, and is raised very seriously. I have had an awful lot of mail on the subject. Some were very good letters. In answering them, we have gotten lawyers and theologians to write about it. It is perfectly clear that although our Christian tradition honors law and would honor the process to change the law rather than to resist it, it is also clear that to make the law absolute is to make it an idol, and you don't do that in place of God. This is what Martin Niemöller was saying in shorter words, but I am doing the German complications of it now!

"The real point of this, I concluded after several months, was that I didn't have any time for it anymore. I didn't have one Negro write the question; I had white people writing the question. The point was that it was lack of imagination on our part. No one who can imagine what it is and has been to be a Negro in Mississippi or Alabama could raise the question in theory, for part of the fact is that there is no way to change the law. The fact is that the law in Negro experience is an instrument of injustice. This is a part of the problem of the whole matter. And this is not altogether confined to Mississippi and Alabama. The fact is that the law can be, unless we have the eternal vigilance that is the price of liberty, oppressive to the poor, not quite the same thing before a judge if you are one of those who is in a group (and I'm not talking about color here at all, I am just talking about whether you are one of the society or one of those who is in difficulty with society).

"Therefore, I think for those of us who prize order, the only answer to this is: O.K., don't easily break the law, don't encourage the flouting of law, but be sure that the law and its practice where you are is an instrument of justice as far as your influence will make it. I am convinced that the responsibility for any violence that is caused by the breaking of the law—and it is catching—is not with those who peacefully demonstrate against injustice, but the ultimate responsibility is with those who persist in letting tradition hold up the equality of injustice for which the law is designed in our tradition to protect."

There was firm applause when Dr. Blake finished his remarks, but Dr. Somerville, stressing the truth that even he, "loyal subject of Queen Elizabeth," agreed to that, referred to the question once again: "It does, however, say, 'Who determines at what point?'"

Dr. Blake continued: "May I refer to our Alliance of Reformed Churches—there are others than Presbyterians and Reformed here, I know. We took this question up several years ago when the sit-ins began. I happened to be chairman of a committee on religious liberty. We discussed what religious liberty was, but it was perfectly clear that traditionally Calvinists have been mixed up in most of the revolutions that have gone on for the last four hundred and fifty years.

"Now part of the reason that we were so unanimous is that there were a lot of Scotch-Irish here, too. They didn't like anything English, and therefore not only their ethics but also their racial feelings enabled them to be quite happy about entering it. And I think of you, Martin. One of the earliest words that I was taught to think of very badly is 'Hessian,' for they were mercenary troops that King George used to try to fight George Washington in Trenton, but they drank too much on Christmas Eve and were defeated.

"Now, what we concluded together in our group was in essence this: A group of Christians, after discussion with the brethren, decides this is the way to do it rather than to set oneself up as an individual judge. This is a part of what the church does in a community; so, it is not a

man on his own, necessarily. At least if the Christian
church is what it is, and he is Christian, there ought to
be more than one, there ought to be several rallying
about the problem. We must understand what we are
doing and know we must do this. We must obey God
rather than man.

"However, there is a problem, our main problem as
Christians. I freely admit it, especially when I am talking
to my secular friends. We confuse ourselves with God
rather than trying to be obedient to God. And this is a
part of the basic sin."

At this point, more than one hour had elapsed since
these discussions had begun. As question after question
was read, the group listened with fascination to the answers, impromptu though they were. We could have
gone on much longer, but time was running out. The
final set of questions and the replies provided sufficient
food for thought to be taken into the morrow.

Dr. Somerville: "Dr. Niemöller, we have two questions
here now. One is specifically addressed to you and one is
addressed both to you and to Dr. Blake. I'll read the
question to you first and then I'll give the other one to
Dr. Blake, who may comment on it then. Dr. Niemöller,
'Could you give your estimate of the comparative serious-
ness of Nazism and Communism as challenges to the Christian church in your generation?'"

Dr. Niemöller: "Nazism is far more serious and a greater
danger to the Christian church than Communism could
ever be. Everybody knows that Communism is atheistic,
propagates atheism, is against the church and against
Christianity; whereas Adolf Hitler announced in his party's
platform—it was point number twenty-four—that national
socialism recognized and was based upon what he called

'Positive Christianity.' This statement brought thousands
and thousands of Christians into the fold who believed
that this new party with its great ideals would bring about
a drastic change, a betterment of living conditions as they
then existed in Germany. Not until the Nazis seized the
power did these people begin to understand that Adolf
Hitler and his party would be the ones to determine that
positive Christianity would henceforth be interpreted by
Hitler's ideas, thoughts, and intentions. These people
joined the party because they felt that in order to be
positive Christians they must become Nazis. These people
were tempted and misled, and such a thing cannot happen
as far as Communism is concerned. Communism attacks,
Nazism tempted. The temptation always is much more
dangerous than the attack."

Dr. Somerville asked Dr. Blake to comment on that
subject if he cared to. Then he read the final question:
" 'In regard to the subject of Wednesday's service, will
you each speak about the recognition of Red China in
the United Nations?' "

"The question is a good one, a very important one,"
Dr. Blake said. "We'll not get out of the swamp in Vietnam
until it is handled; after all, how long do Americans think
we can go on as if seven hundred million Chinese on the
mainland do not exist? I recognize, as most anybody does
in public life, that this is a subject that apparently the
United States citizen is not willing at the present even to
discuss. Several years ago, when a rather able conference
of the National Council of Churches made up of theologians and people who are experts on foreign affairs (it
was not a representative church consultation) was discussing the matter, there was one little sentence in a
hundred-page report that said no more than I have already
said.

"This ought to be examined because things are not going very well in Asia for us. It was taken up by people who wanted to attack the church and the National Council of Churches, and before any of our constituency had read the report or even heard about it, the National Council of Churches was damned as being infiltrated by Communists.

"Now, all I say is that I have heard more questions raised in good thinking about this subject among officials who are stuck with the situation at the present moment. Don't misunderstand me, please. The mere inviting of Communist China in the United Nations, our willingness to abstain or to vote for them, does not begin to solve the problem. About as far as I can go is to say this: If we want to go on ignoring this reality—we talk about controlling atomic energy!—what on earth are we thinking about if we aren't thinking about somehow getting the Chinese nation now, which has the beginnings of this atomic power, included in the responsibilities and the control that the community of nations means?

"I know we have commitments to Chiang Kai-shek. We have commitments to the Philippines and other peoples who are terribly afraid for us to change our policy at all. I hope that we will be willing to make this clear whenever there is any real opportunity to discuss it with those who are behind the problem in Southeast Asia. And, as far as I know, I think we are ready to talk whenever there is anybody willing to talk to us. This at least I have heard from government officials. But, I would remind you that in most of the world our policy does not look very bright!"

"Dr. Niemöller?" Dr. Somerville asked. His reply was the final one this evening, and it concluded the wealth of the discussions of our great week. Though it was to the point, it also placed clearly before us the question marks that continue to be affixed to all sorts and conditions of men. "No," he said, "I do not like to speak to this because my own country, my two Germanys, are not members of the United Nations and are not even allowed to appeal for membership. In the Declaration of Sovereignty, this right has been kept by what formerly were the occupation powers and now are our friendly guests."

This was the end. Dr. Somerville, a perfect master of ceremonies, had this to say, pleasantly and regretfully: "We have more questions here, though they by and large cover the same areas. It is a terrific strain on our friends to go on in this manner; it is much more difficult for them than a prepared script, and I think the hour is come when we must bid them a reluctant farewell."

At this, the appreciation of the people became manifest in renewed applause, which continued through the word of thanks that Dr. Somerville extended to our great friends for what they had given us this evening and throughout the days of the week. It continued as an accompaniment to Dr. Somerville's (anxious) question: "Do you think there are enough Presbyterians here that we might strike up the Doxology?" and to Dr. Pratt's thanking Dr. Somerville and his people "for the setting up of this very fine termination point."

And then we arose and placed our thanks where it all belongs:

"Praise God from whom all blessings flow,

Praise Him, all creatures here below;

Praise Him above, ye heavenly host:

Praise Father, Son, and Holy Ghost. Amen."

EPILOGUE

EPILOGUE

There was an air of gratefulness in the singing of the Doxology. Our week had come to its end. We went away, gained distance, looked back, and began to ponder.

The week had come to an end, but it was not over by any means. For days after, strangers spoke to me in the street to say how much this week had done for them, for their faith. Friends expressed it, too. Lovie Welch, managing the busiest lunch counter at the corner drugstore for endless hours every day, had broken away to attend, with her sister and helper Betty, just one time, Monday. "I cannot begin to tell you how newly inspired I am," she said, juggling four cups of coffee without spilling a drop. "It has given me new peace, inner calm —yes, and strength!"

Two other friends contemplated the impact of the week on Philadelphia. Joan Hemenway was certain that the entire city gained a great deal from such an opportunity. Betty Moyer felt that even William Penn himself would have appreciated this great event.

There could be no doubt that people were newly inspired. Inspired not just within themselves but as human beings who had worshiped together for a week and under the tremendous challenge of the things that were said had become a new family, a family in Christ; and they were aware of it.

The things that were said actually spoke to the people and touched them. From the beginning there was an intense response manifest each day in the clear, strong, common recitation of the Creed and the Lord's Prayer and, indeed, in glorious and spirited singing of all hymns. The people wanted to take their part.

The things that were said were well summarized in an article by Kay Longcope in *Presbyterian Life* in mid-April, 1965, from which I quote:

Dr. Niemöller and Dr. Blake ranged over the most crucial issues now before the modern Christian church—those of unity, race relations, poverty, the church's role in politics and economics, and evangelism. They left no doubt in the minds of nearly three thousand persons who heard their talks that the world now expects every Christian and his church to take the initiative in a conflict-filled universe to help build a worldwide society in which there is universal concern about one's neighbor, whether he is black or white or in-between, . . . lives around the corner or a continent away.

The things that were said caused us to ponder, to probe our reactions. The Reverend Elizabeth W. Fenske gave this evaluation:

During the week it was truly stimulating to contemplate, exchange ideas, and plot new directions under the guidance and leadership of two committed ecumenical leaders.

The week provided a challenge which we need more often as we seek to be concerned with relevant issues facing Christians in the twentieth century.

Her husband, the Reverend Paul B. Fenske, had this to say:

The greatest and most lifting experience of life is to be in the presence of men and women whose lives are testaments of their faith. So it was with expectancy that we came to hear and to be challenged by the words of Martin Niemöller and Eugene Carson Blake and by the lives behind those words. It was to address the church in twentieth-century Philadelphia that they had come—to talk of its mission and its call to be faithful to Jesus Christ. We looked forward to hearing a contemporary interpretation of the message written to the early congregation in Philadephia and to hearing of the task that lies beyond the "open door."

That this anticipation was fulfilled is made amply clear by the spirit of the events of the week and by the content of the sermon-dialogues.

The things that were said caused various reactions in various persons. We can relate but a few here:

I think the Niemöller-Blake dialogue was one of the more exciting things that has happened in Philadelphia this year. It was an eloquent call for the razing of the barriers of denominationalism and parochialism, for the conversion of all of us from churchmanship to discipleship.

Thus wrote the Reverend H. Francis Hines, the director of the Department of Broadcasting of the Philadelphia Council of Churches. He arranged for an hour-long conversation between the two men in which they summarized all that was said during the week. A local station teletaped it.

Harry E. Ott, the secretary-treasurer of the Philadelphia Association of the United Church of Christ, gave this testimony:

I was able to attend every one of the five sessions and found them to be inspirational, very stimulating, as well as thought-provoking. Indeed, the hour of 5:15 P.M. was most convenient for any center city employed person to reach the church. The choice of the theme hymn has left an impression that will remain with me always. . . . Indeed, it was a richly rewarding experience in thinking through the "cost and joy of discipleship" in the age in which we live. I cannot think of one possible criticism, except the shortness of the time each evening.

The Reverend Philip W. Weiss, the pastor of Bethany United Church of Christ, had one regret. He told me that he derived a great deal of benefit from the dialogues, so much so that he should have liked to share this with many more people than were there. Although the church was comfortably filled each day, he wished for S.R.O. congregations, and of course he was not alone in that. For what all of us could gain day by day, as individuals as well as a family of people, was nothing short of a Pentecost.

Dr. Moyer, our publicity chairman, gave his time and talents to our planning and preparing, even though simultaneously he planned and prepared a series of meetings for all four Sundays in February in his own church. They were called "University for Living" and dealt with the aspects of "the city we live in." All the more we are grateful for his involvement that caused him to say this:

For my part, this was a dynamically personal adventure in Christian friendship. In terms of depth and inclusiveness, it has been the most authentically ecumenical experience I have been privileged to share in over a decade of ministry in the City of Brotherly Love. Many of my people and our good neighbors are saying their own resounding "Amen" to the grateful reaction I express. Our witness has the more spine and muscle to it for having spent those five memorable nights together.

There was one deeply personal reaction—yet part of our search for unity—that I share with you. It came from a dear friend of mine, the Reverend Brian Kingslake. He is

British born and serves his Lord as a pastor of the Church of the New Jerusalem, the Swedenborgians. I met him and his wife, Jill, in South Africa many years ago when they were serving, untiringly and under great difficulties, among those whom our sin has made to be "the least of Christ's brethren."

Brian gave the benediction on Wednesday night. And later he said to me:

You know, in a lifetime of service this is the first time that I was permitted to pronounce the benediction from an Episcopal altar!

Finally then, the things that were said remain with us as the reminder of the challenge they were intended to be: "The Challenge to the Church." Will we now look back to that unique experience as to something that we have enjoyed, or will we with joy arrive at a new commitment to live and to act our faith in Jesus Christ?

"The things that were said, please sum them up for me," I asked my friend, Dr. Longley, the general chairman. He did so in these words:

That is simple enough. The theme persevering through the week was that we live in the day of the revolution of man. This revolution could go either way: if evil, man will lose; if good, man will win. The open-door Christian will see to it that the revolution goes the Christian way—through churches and through individuals. The church is above the world, yet in the world. The church is the extension of the incarnation, it is the body of Christ. In the midst of the world's culture, the Christian way is the transforming, redeeming, saving way for man in all the areas of life. This is what the men talked about.

This is what the men talked about; these are the things that were said. We heard no intellectual dissertations on spiritual subjects: we heard the Word of God. When it was all said and done, we marveled at the gift we had received. The "Issues and Opportunities Facing the Church of Jesus Christ" ultimately led to one simple equation, namely, "Facing Jesus Christ."

"Hold fast what you have, so that no one may seize your crown." We, the people of that week, wish to share it with you. And we have told the story, thinking of that "love, which binds everything together in perfect harmony."